Teh FEB 6 1997

DEMCO

EXPERIMENTING WITH SCIENCE IN SPORTS

OTHER BOOKS by Robert Gardner

EXPERIMENTING WITH ENERGY CONSERVATION
EXPERIMENTING WITH ILLUSIONS
EXPERIMENTING WITH INVENTIONS
EXPERIMENTING WITH LIGHT
EXPERIMENTING WITH SOUND
FAMOUS EXPERIMENTS YOU CAN DO
IDEAS FOR SCIENCE PROJECTS
MORE IDEAS FOR SCIENCE PROJECTS
ROBERT GARDNER'S FAVORITE
        SCIENCE EXPERIMENTS
SCIENCE EXPERIMENTS

EXPERIMENTING WITH SCIENCE IN SPORTS

BY ROBERT GARDNER

FRANKLIN WATTS
NEW YORK   CHICAGO   LONDON   TORONTO   SYDNEY
A VENTURE BOOK

Photographs copyright ©: Photo Researchers, Inc., NYC: pp. 19 (Gerard
Vandystadt), 106 (Tim Davis), 116 (Jerry Wachter); Education Development
Center: pp. 32, 33; Comstock, Inc.: p. 41; UPI/Bettmann Newsphotos: pp. 50,
55, 70, 95.

Library of Congress Cataloging-in-Publication Data

Gardner, Robert, 1929–
    Experimenting with science in sports / by Robert Gardner.
       p. cm. — (A Venture book)
    Includes bibliographical references (p.) and index.
    Summary: Discusses how such principles of physics as force,
gravity, and momentum apply to a variety of athletic actions, with
experiments for the reader to try.
       ISBN 0-531-12543-2
    1. Science—Experiments—Juvenile literature. 2. Physics—
Experiments—Juvenile literature. 3. Sports—Juvenile literature.
[1. Science—Experiments. 2. Physics—Experiments. 3. Experiments.
4. Sports.] I. Title.
Q164.G318 1993
507.8—dc20   92-37994 CIP AC

CONTENTS

EXPERIMENTING WITH SCIENCE IN SPORTS

"LET THE GAMES BEGIN"

If you enjoy both sports and science and if you like to perform experiments, this book should appeal to you. You'll find that a variety of athletic actions offer opportunities for experimentation—experimentation that will help you to better understand both the action and the science behind it. For example, you may have heard a sports announcer say, "That throw from the outfield 'hung in the air' too long; the runner had no difficulty scoring from second on that base hit." By "hung in the air," the broadcaster means that the fielder's throw followed an arc rather than moving along a path closer to a straight line. In Chapter 3, you'll have a chance to experiment with a variety of throws to see how a ball's time of flight is related to the angle at which it is thrown. This experiment is but one of the many investigations you'll carry out in *Experimenting with Science in Sports*.

In the pages that follow, you'll find experiments that involve running, jumping, throwing, and batting. There are experiments that deal with athletic footwear and friction; spinning, curving, and bouncing balls; air resistance; the levers used in sports; ways to measure and reduce air resistance in athletic events; and investigations that show how the laws of motion and conservation of energy and momentum apply to sports. These and many more experiments and research projects will keep both your mind and body active for many hours.

The level of difficulty of the experiments and the questions for research projects varies. Some are quite straightforward and easy to do. Others are quite challenging and require careful preparation, thought, and analysis. However, you do not have to do all the experiments, nor do you have to do most of them in any particular order. Choose the ones that you find interesting, but keep in mind that you can learn a lot about science and the way it's done by choosing at least one or more experiments and projects that challenge your mind and skills—experiments that require you to think deeply; experiments that lead to results you find perplexing. Only by striving to understand those things that you find difficult can you develop your thinking and reasoning skills to their fullest. If you choose to meet such challenges, you'll find that your self-esteem will improve as much as your grasp of science and scientific techniques.

As a former science teacher and coach, I have always taken great delight in the many scientific laws and principles that can be observed on, or in, athletic fields, courts, rinks, and pools. Although it was not always easy to bring these principles to the attention of the young athletes I coached, I found that using illustrations from sports to explain scientific concepts invariably generated enthusiasm in the classroom and laboratory. Sometimes it even generated enthusiasm for learning!

The experiments that you'll find here, like the sports from which they arise, require measurements. In some cases, the measurements involve metric units, which are widely used in science, in Olympic sports, and in most countries throughout the world. In others, the English units commonly found in baseball, football, and other American sports are used. Because the English unit for mass, the *slug,* is so seldom used, all masses will be measured in kilograms. Occasionally, the pound will appear as a unit of force, but usually forces will be measured in newtons.

The tables below contain all the units you will need for the experiments described here. You may also find them useful in converting units within or between the metric and English systems.

Conversion Tables for Units of Measurement Used in Experiments

Time (for both Metric and English)
1.0 hour (h) = 60 minutes (min) = 3600 seconds (s)
1.0 min = 60 s

LENGTH

Metric
1.0 kilometer (km) = 1000 meter (m)
1.0 m = 100 centimeters (cm)
1.0 cm = 10 millimeters (mm)
Metric to English
1.0 m = 3.28 ft = 1.09 yd
1.0 cm = 0.394 in
1.0 km = 0.62 mi

English
1.0 mile (mi) = 1760 yards (yd) = 5280 feet (ft)
1.0 yd = 3.0 ft = 36 inches (in)
1.0 ft = 12 in
English to Metric
1.0 ft = 0.305 m = 30.5 cm
1.0 in = 2.54 cm = 0.0254 m
1.0 mi = 1.61 km

SPEED OR VELOCITY

Metric
1.0 km/h (kph) = 1000 m/s
1.0 m/s = 100 cm/s
Metric to English
1.0 kph = 0.62 mph
1.0 m/s = 1.09 yd/s = 3.28 ft/s

English
1.0 mi/h (mph) = 1.47 ft/s
1.0 ft/s = 12 in/s = 0.68 mph
English to Metric
1.0 mph = 1.61 kph
1.0 ft/s = 0.305 m/s = 30.5 cm/s

VOLUME

Metric
1.0 cubic meter (m^3) = 1,000,000 cubic centimeters (cm^3)
1.0 liter (L) = 1,000 milliliters (mL)

English
1.0 cubic yard (yd^3) = 27 cubic feet (ft^3)

1.0 ft^3 = 1728 in^3

VOLUME (continued)

1.0 gallon (gal) = 4.0 quarts
(qt) = 231 in^3
1.0 qt = 2 pints (pt)

Metric to English
1.0 m^3 = 1.30 yd^3 = 35.3 ft^3
1.0 m^3 = 35.3 ft^3
1.0 cm^3 = .061 in^3

English to Metric
1.0 yd^3 = 0.76 m^3
1.0 ft^3 = 0.028 m^3
1.0 in^3 = 16.4 cm^3

MASS

Metric
1.0 kilogram (kg) = 1000 grams (g)

FORCE (WEIGHT)

Metric
1.0 newton (N) = 100,000
dynes (dyn)
Metric to English
1.0 N = 0.22 lb

English
1.0 pound (lb) = 16 ounces
(oz)
English to Metric
1.0 lb = 4.45 N = 445,000 dyn

WORK OR ENERGY

Metric
1.0 N × 1.0 m = 1.0 N-m =
1.0 joule (J)
Metric to English
1.0 J = 0.74 ft-lb

English
1.0 lb × 1.0 ft = 1.0 ft-lb

English to Metric
1.0 ft-lb = 1.36 J

1

ATHLETES ON THE MOVE: FROM FLYING FEET TO ROTATING LEVERS

"It's the only sport lasting more than two minutes that starts with an all-out sprint." Crew, as described by Fritz Hagerman (Ohio University)

In this chapter you'll have an opportunity to look at the way human running speeds vary with the distance of the race. You may also choose to investigate whether or not there are limits to the records established in various events; explore whether it's to your advantage to be left-handed in baseball; experiment with friction in athletic footwear and the nature of the surface on which such shoes are used; examine the effect of wind direction on discus throws, and learn how a simple machine is used in some sports. We'll begin with a look at human running speeds in various races.

HUMAN SPEED OVER VARYING DISTANCES

Have you ever noticed that distance runners tend to be thin and wiry? Sprinters, on the other hand, are often stocky, with thick heavy calves and thighs. Perhaps these differences have to do with the way they run. Table 1 lists some men's and women's Olympic world record times for running events of different lengths. What happens to the average speed of these record-setting runners as the length of the race increases?

Table 1. Olympic World Records

Men		Women	
Event	Time	Event	Time
100 m	9.92 s	100 m	10.54 s
200 m	19.75 s	200 m	21.34 s
400 m	43.8 s	400 m	48.65 s
800 m	1 min, 43.00 s	800 m	1 min, 53.5 s
1,500 m	3 min, 32.53 s	1,500 m	3 min, 53.96 s
5,000 m	13 min, 5.59 s		
10,000 m	27 min, 21.46 s		

Of course, you or your friends probably can't run at the record-setting speeds shown in Table 1. However, you can run different distances, with or without competition. Use a stopwatch to determine the time for each distance you run. Then calculate the

16

average running speed for each distance. What happens to your average speed as the distance of the run increases? How does your speed compare with those of the Olympic record-setters?

QUESTIONS FOR FURTHER RESEARCH

- Look closely at the record times for the men's 100 m and 200 m events. How do the average speeds for these two events compare? In which event did the record-holder run faster? Do you find similar results from your own running experiments? How can you explain these surprising results?

  You might begin by investigating when a runner reaches his or her maximum speed after starting from rest. Is maximum speed reached instantaneously, or does it require some time? If it takes some time, how would you determine the runner's average acceleration from start (speed = 0) to maximum speed?

- As mentioned above, long-distance runners are frequently thin, whereas sprinters are usually muscular with thick, heavy thighs and calves. How can you explain these differences in body structure?

- What do runners mean when they speak of *carbohydrate loading?*

- Examine the records established in a number of other Olympic events. In what sport do athletes develop the highest speeds? Can you explain why swimmers move so slowly in comparison with other athletes?

- How do the speeds of racehorses, greyhounds, and human runners compare?

RECORDS ARE MADE TO BE BROKEN

Until the middle of the twentieth century, many people thought that no one would ever run the mile in less than four minutes. They believed that surpassing the four-minute barrier required a speed beyond human capability. Then, in 1954, Roger Bannister showed that the long-established four-minute barrier could be surmounted when he ran a mile in 3 minutes, 59.4 seconds. Today, it is not unusual to see a race in which all the competitors run the mile in less than four minutes.

Many of today's athletes, bursting with confidence as new records are established every year, claim that there are no limits to the speeds, distances, lengths, and heights that athletes can run, throw, and jump. Do you agree?

You might enjoy examining the times for various Olympic events since 1900. You can find the winning times, distances, lengths, and heights for a wide variety of events in a world almanac. Your school or local library probably has a copy. In which event or events does there seem to have been the greatest change in winning time, distance, length, or height? In which event or events does there seem to have been the least change? How can you explain the variation in the rate that winning times, distances, lengths, and heights have changed for different events? In the pole vault, for example, can you see the effect of the more flexible fiberglass poles introduced in the early 1960s?

Use a sports record book to determine the rate of increase over time in the world record for pole vaulting. Is there any correlation with the introduction of fiberglass poles?

If you plot a graph of winning time, distance, length, or height for the various events against a time axis running from 1900 to the present, what does the slope of the graph indicate? If you extrapolate (extend) the graphs, do any of them seem to indicate a limiting barrier? Do any of the graphs reveal what might have been considered to be a barrier—a barrier that was later broken?

A QUESTION FOR FURTHER RESEARCH

• Some people claim that women athletes are improving at a faster rate than men are. Can you find evidence to support or refute such claims?

DO LEFTIES HAVE AN ADVANTAGE?

Left-handed people frequently claim that society discriminates against them. Scissors, can openers, lawn mowers, one-armed writing desks, as well as the process of writing itself, are among the many items and processes that seem to have been designed for right-handed people. However, there seems to be some evidence for believing that left-handers have an advantage in baseball. From 1946 to 1989, 55 of the 88 major-league batting championships were won by left-handed batters. Left-handers scored better despite the fact that nearly twice as many major league players (as viewed by the pitcher) bat from the right side of the plate as from the left side.

To investigate one possible reason for this statistic, you'll need a stopwatch, a bat, a 90-foot-long base path (or its equivalent), and a tireless friend who likes to run. Ask your friend to assume the stance of a right-handed batter and swing at an imaginary pitch as it crosses the plate and then run as fast as he or she can to first base. As your friend's bat crosses home plate, start your stopwatch. Stop the watch when your friend steps on first base. How long did it take him or her to run from home to first after hitting the imaginary ball?

Wait several minutes and have your friend repeat the experiment from a left-handed stance while you again measure the time required for your friend to run from home to first. Repeat this experiment several times and, if possible, with different people since your friend may not be tireless after all. How do the times to reach first base from home compare for right-handed batters vs. left-handed batters? Can you explain any time difference that you discover?

QUESTIONS FOR FURTHER RESEARCH

- What factors might explain the predominance of left-handers in winning batting championships?
- In the general population the ratio of right-handed people to left-handed people is 9 to 1. What is the ratio of right-handed batters to left-handed batters in major league baseball? The ratio of right-handed pitchers to left-handed pitchers? How do these ratios in baseball compare with those of the population in general? Can you explain why?
- What statistics might you collect to see if the predominance of left-handedness in baseball is justified?
- Why are left-handed catchers, third basemen,

shortstops, or second basemen not found on major league rosters?

ATHLETIC FOOTWEAR AND FRICTION

There are athletic shoes for every sport. Some have cleats, some are smooth, some are rough, and some are so filled with holes that the soles resemble the surface of the moon. If you've ever tried to walk on a freshly waxed floor in leather-soled shoes, you know there is very little friction. In the next experiment you'll investigate how friction is related to the kind of shoe you wear.

Place a leather-soled shoe on a smooth wood or tile-covered floor or table. Add some weight, such as a heavy book, to the shoe so that it rests firmly against the surface. Tape one end of a string to the front of the shoe. Attach the other end to a sensitive spring scale. Measure the force needed to pull the shoe along the surface at a slow but steady speed. What is the frictional force between the shoe and the surface?

Now repeat the experiment with an athletic shoe—a running shoe, for example. What is the frictional force between the athletic shoe and the surface? How does it compare with the frictional force of the leather-soled shoe and the surface?

QUESTIONS FOR FURTHER RESEARCH

• How does weight affect the friction between two surfaces? If you double the weight, does the friction double? Would a heavier basketball player be less likely to slip than a lighter one?

- How does the surface area of the shoe affect friction? You might find out by spreading the same weight over two shoes instead of one. Don't forget to include the weight of the shoes! How does the increased surface area affect the force of friction?
- Does the kind of surface over which the shoe moves affect friction? Is the friction between shoe and wood the same as that between shoe and vinyl tile? How about other surfaces?
- Measure the friction between wood and as many types of athletic shoes as you can assemble. Which types of shoes seem to provide the most friction on wood?
- A pitcher sometimes goes to the rosin bag and spreads the powder over his or her hand. If you spread rosin over the surface of a shoe, how does it affect the friction between the shoe and a given surface?
- How do shoes designed for play on artificial turf differ from those worn on real grass-covered soil? Why are they different?

TRACK HARDNESS AND SPEED

The friction between a runner's shoes and the surface enables him or her to push off and run effectively. As you may know from having tried to walk on an icy path, a runner can't move without friction. But given the normal friction between the proper athletic shoes and cinders, grass, artificial turf, asphalt, boards, or whatever, many athletes claim that they can run faster on some surfaces than on others. Some professional football players prefer artificial turf; they claim that they can generate more speed on turf than on natural grass. You can test this idea experimentally.

Ask a friend to run *in place* on a sidewalk or lawn for two minutes. Tell that person to run at what he or she considers a fast steady pace while you count the number of steps taken. Then, after a five-minute rest, ask the same person to run at the same pace on a pair of large thick cushions. What happens to the person's actual pace in terms of number of steps taken per minute? How do you think an exceptionally soft track would affect a runner's speed?

Ask a number of people, one at a time, to each run half a mile as fast as possible on a number of different level surfaces. You might try soft turf, hard turf, packed cinders, asphalt, wood, sand, pine needles, and any other surfaces that are available. The runners should obtain sufficient rest between runs so that they are not tired at the start of any one of the half-mile runs.

Try to predict ahead of time the track on which you think the runners will achieve the fastest times and the slowest times. After all the data has been collected, what did you find was the fastest track? The slowest? Can you explain why?

WIND AND THE DISCUS

Any runner or cyclist will tell you that it's much easier to run with the wind at your back rather than in your face. Similarly, punters, passers, and place kickers in football like to kick or throw with rather than against the wind. However, some baseball pitchers and discus throwers prefer to throw into the wind. Discus throwers often claim that they can throw the discus farther if they throw it against the wind.

To check these claims, ask several discus throwers to make some practice throws on several windy days during the track season. Do they make longer throws against the wind rather than with the wind? If so, is there some particular wind speed that seems to produce maximum results?

How can you explain the results of these experiments? How do discus throwers explain the effect of the wind on their results?

LEVERS, SPEED, AND SPORTS

The great Greek mathematician Archimedes is reported to have said, "Give me a place to stand on and I will move the earth." His boast was based on the principle of the lever, which he had studied as a mathematician and used as an engineer.

A lever is a simple machine consisting of a bar that rotates about a fixed point called the fulcrum—the axis about which the bar turns. There are three types or classes of levers, which are illustrated in Figure 1a. In all the levers shown, f is the fulcrum about which the lever rotates; W is the weight or load force to be moved by the lever; and E is the effort force, or the force that is applied to make the load move. The distance from the fulcrum to the load, D_W, is called the lever arm of the load; the distance from the fulcrum to the effort, D_E, is the lever arm of the effort force.

The lever arm of any force is the perpendicular distance between the force and the fulcrum. The mo-

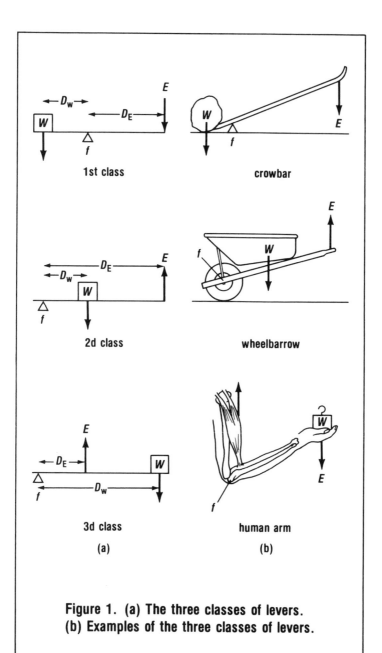

Figure 1. (a) The three classes of levers.
(b) Examples of the three classes of levers.

ment of a force is defined as the product of the force and the lever arm. In Figure 1a, $D_E \times E$ is the counterclockwise moment of the force about the fulcrum E; $D_W \times W$ is the clockwise moment.

When a lever is balanced (not rotating), the moment of force tending to cause a clockwise rotation equals the moment of force tending to cause a counterclockwise rotation. For each of the three classes of levers shown, $D_E \times E = D_W \times W$ when the levers are at equilibrium. When the moment of the effort force exceeds the moment of the load force, the load will begin to move.

As you can see from the diagrams, with first-class and second-class levers a large load can be moved with an effort force that is smaller than the load as long as D_E is greater than D_W. In the case of third-class levers, the effort force must always exceed the load for the desired movement to occur. For example, the biceps muscle shown in Figure 1b must exert a force E that is at least D_W/D_E times greater than W to hold the load in place. On the other hand, the load on a third-class lever can be made to move much faster than the point at which the effort force is applied. In fact, when the lever rotates, the ratio of the speed of the load to the speed of the effort force will be the ratio of the two lever arms:

$$\frac{V_W}{V_E} = \frac{D_W}{D_E}$$

Examine some of the levers used in sports—fishing poles, lacrosse sticks, hockey sticks, and the oar used to row a crew shell. To which class do each of these levers belong? How does the effort

27

force in each case compare with the load when the levers are in equilibrium? When the effort force moves, how does its speed compare with the speed of the load in each case?

Can the rackets used in tennis, racquetball, and squash be classified as levers? How about baseball bats? If they are levers, where are their fulcrums?

QUESTIONS FOR FURTHER RESEARCH

- Baseball coaches sometimes use fungo bats to hit flies and grounders to fielders. What is a fungo bat? Why do coaches prefer fungo bats to ordinary baseball bats for hitting baseballs? Does it have anything to do with levers?
- In lacrosse, the length of the stick used varies with position. Is this related to leverage, or are there other reasons?

2

MOTION AND SPORTS: GETTING THINGS MOVING

Sports fact: The downward velocity of a diver increases at a rate of 9.8 m/s every second. At the end of a ten-meter dive, the diver touches the water with a speed of 14 m/s (30 mph) after falling for 1.42 s.

Any athletic game or activity involves motion; consequently, to understand much of the science that underlies sports requires a knowledge of the three laws of motion. Fortunately, playing sports is a good way to learn about them firsthand.

GETTING STARTED: SPORTS AND THE LAWS OF MOTION

To make any object or being move or change its velocity, a force must be applied. Without a force, the object or body will simply remain at rest or move with constant velocity. To make a bowling ball that is at rest on an alley floor start rolling, you must give it a push or a pull. The push or pull that you apply is a force. If you wanted, you could attach a spring scale to the ball and measure the size of the force you exert. To make a baseball, basketball, shot put, or discus move, you generally use your hand and arm to provide a force. A football or soccer ball may be put into motion by forces applied with your foot. Bats and rackets are used to exert forces on tennis balls and baseballs.

When a force is applied to an object, the object accelerates, that is, its velocity changes. Once the force is removed, the object will move at a constant velocity. Of course, if you try to push a heavy box along a floor, the box won't move at all unless you apply a large force because another force—friction—opposes the force you apply. Again, once you stop pushing, the box will quickly come to rest because the frictional force pushes against the motion.

To see what happens when frictional forces are small, use a hockey stick to apply a force to a puck resting on clean, smooth ice near one end of a pond or hockey rink. (If you don't have access to a frozen pond or an ice rink, do similar experiments on an air-hockey table, or examine the experiments shown in the photographs that follow.) After you have hit the puck, you'll see it move quite uniformly along the ice. Some friends armed with stopwatches can measure the puck's speed at different times after you launch it. Place some markers, separated by equal distances, along the ice beyond the point where you shoot the puck. Have one person measure the time it takes the puck to move from marker 1 to marker 2. Have another person measure the time for the puck to move from marker 1 to marker 3; another from marker 1 to marker 4. Begin by launching the puck with a fairly small force. If it takes the puck 5.0 seconds to move between a pair of markers that are 10 m apart, then its average speed between those two markers is

$$\frac{10 \text{ m}}{5.0 \text{ s}} = 2.0 \text{ m/s.}$$

(If the markers are 10 yards apart and the time is the same, the average speed is 2 yards per second or 6 feet per second.)

How does the speed over the second interval compare with the speed over the first? How does the speed over the third interval compare with the speed over the second interval? Over the first interval?

The friction between a dry-ice puck, like the one seen in the photograph on page 32, and the plate glass on which it rests is very small. In an experiment using a dry-ice puck like the one shown, the puck was given a push. Then, as it moved beside a meter stick, a picture was taken from above at 0.42-second intervals. As you can see, the puck moved almost exactly the same distance (14 cm) during each time interval. This experiment, like the one with a hockey puck, illustrates Newton's first law of motion: A body in motion maintains its speed and direction of motion unless acted upon by an outside force. If the body's velocity is zero, then it remains at rest unless . . .

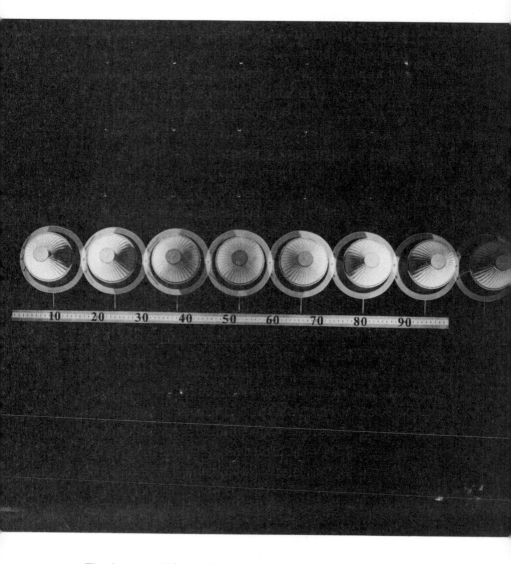

The force on this moving dry-ice puck is practically zero because there is very little friction between the puck and the glass on which it is sliding. As you can see, the puck moves with a constant velocity.

Repeat the experiment with the hockey puck, but this time apply a larger force to the puck. How does the puck's speed compare with its speed in the first experiment?

Try the experiment again after skaters have produced a thin layer of "snow" and before the ice is cleaned. Why does the puck's velocity decrease more rapidly than it did before?

You've seen that the puck moves faster when the force applied to it is greater. You've seen too that the puck's speed decreases more rapidly when it moves against a retarding force (snow). In a more carefully controlled experiment, shown in the photographs on page 34, you can see that the force pulling the puck in the top picture is supplied by a rubber ring. The ring is stretched by a fixed amount so as to keep the force constant. In both pictures, a flash bulb illuminated the pucks every 0.42 s. Careful measurements of the top picture show that the distance the puck traveled increased by about 2.4 cm with every succeeding flash. With this information, its change in velocity between flashes can be calculated:

$$\Delta V = \frac{\Delta d}{\Delta t} = \frac{2.4\text{cm}}{0.42\text{s}} = 5.7 \text{ cm/s. (The symbol, } \Delta\text{, means } \textit{change in.}\text{)}$$

Since its velocity increased by 5.7 cm/s between flashes (an interval of 0.42 s), its acceleration, that is, its change in velocity per unit time is

$$a = \frac{5.7 \text{ cm/s}}{0.42 \text{ s}} = 14 \text{ cm/s/s, or } 14 \text{ cm/s}^2.$$

In the lower picture you'll find that the puck is being pulled by *two* rubber rings each stretched as

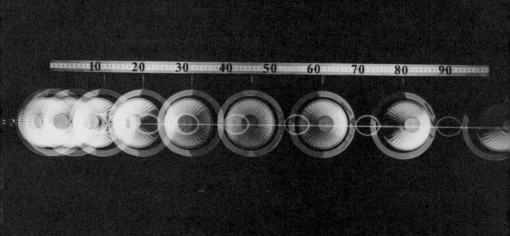

much as the one in the top picture. Therefore, the force acting on the puck in the lower photo is twice as great as before. With this larger force, the velocity increases by about 4.8 cm/flash every flash. How does the acceleration of this puck, in cm/s/s, compare with that of the first puck? When the force on the puck is doubled, what happens to its acceleration?

These experiments illustrate what Sir Isaac Newton discovered more than 300 years ago. The acceleration of an object is proportional to the force applied to it and inversely proportional to the object's mass, which is the amount of matter it contains. The amount of matter in an object can be determined by placing it on one pan of an equal-arm balance. Standard masses are then placed on the other pan until balance is achieved. A baseball, for example, has a mass between 142 and 149 grams (5 and 5.25 ounces) or 0.142 and 0.149 kilogram (kg). An object's mass is the same

Facing page, top: The force on this puck is kept constant. Careful measurements will show that its acceleration (increase in velocity per time) is also constant.

Bottom: As you can see, the force on this puck is twice as great as in the picture on page 32. Careful measurements will show that the acceleration is also twice as great.

everywhere. Its weight, which is the force exerted on the object by gravity, can vary from place to place. For example, an object whose mass is 1 kg will weigh nearly 10 newtons (N) (2.2 lb) on the earth's surface. On the moon, the object will have the same mass, but its weight will be only 1.6 N because the force of gravity on the moon is about one-sixth as great as it is on earth.

Newton's discovery that the acceleration of an object is proportional to the force applied to it and inversely proportional to its mass is known as Newton's second law of motion. It can be summarized by the equation:

$$a = \frac{F}{m} \quad \text{or} \quad F = ma.$$

When the mass is measured in kilograms and the acceleration in meters per second squared, the force is in newtons. Thus, a force of one newton is equal to one kilogram-meter per second squared ($kg\text{-}m/s^2$).

Force (in newtons) = 1 kg × 1 m/s^2 = 1 kg-m/s^2 = 1 N.

If a force of 8 N is applied to a 2-kg mass, the mass will accelerate at 4 m/s^2, provided there is no friction to retard the motion.

$$a = \frac{F}{m} = \frac{8 \text{ N}}{2 \text{ kg}} = \frac{8 \text{ kg-m/s}^2}{2 \text{ kg}} = 4 \text{ m/s}^2.$$

If there is a frictional force of 2 N opposing the motion, then a force of 10 N will be required to give the mass the same acceleration.

Experiments reveal that all bodies falling toward

the earth because of gravity experience the same downward acceleration—g. The value of g near the earth's surface is 9.8 m/s^2. Therefore, the gravitational force on, or the weight of, a body close to the earth is mg. The weight of a 1-kg mass is 1 kg $\times$ 9.8 m/s^2 = 9.8 N. The weight of a 10-kg mass is 98 N. Of course, in many cases the air resistance on a falling body exerts an opposing force that reduces the downward acceleration. In fact, because air resistance increases with velocity, a falling object may eventually reach an acceleration of zero. When the upward force due to air resistance becomes equal to the body's weight, the net force on the body is zero and so the acceleration must be zero as well. See Figure 2.

Sky divers enjoy free-falling for long distances before opening their parachutes, and they may assume spread-eagle positions to increase air resistance. At about 55 m/s (125 mph) the upward force of the air on their bodies is about equal to their weight. When divers reach this velocity, which is called their terminal velocity, they no longer accelerate, but fall at a constant velocity. To accelerate downward again, they can change their body position to one that offers less air resistance and accelerate once more. If they again assume a spread-eagle position, they will actually slow down until they reach the terminal velocity they had before.

THE THIRD LAW OF MOTION

Newton's third law of motion states: "To every action there is always opposed an equal reaction, or the mutual reactions of two bodies upon each other are always

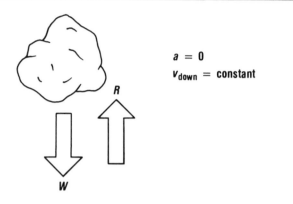

$a = 0$
$v_{down} = $ constant

R

W

Figure 2. When the air resistance pushing on a falling body equals the body's weight, its acceleration becomes zero. It reaches a steady downward speed called its terminal velocity.

equal and directed to contrary directions.'' This simply means that pushes or pulls come in pairs. If you push on something or someone, that object or person automatically pushes back on you. If you push to the right, you receive a push to the left. It's important to remember that the forces are exerted by and on different objects. If you push on a tree, the tree pushes back on you.

Every step you take is an illustration of the third law of motion. You are able to take a step forward because the earth pushes you, and thereby accelerates you, in that direction. The earth pushes you forward because your foot pushes backward against the earth.

Because the earth is so massive, its acceleration in the direction opposite yours is so negligible that only you appear to move. If you've ever tried to step from a small, untied boat onto a dock, your unexpected fall into the water may have made you aware of your equal and opposite force on the boat.

If you try to walk normally on very smooth ice while wearing leather-soled shoes, you won't be able to move forward (or backward) because your foot simply slides; it cannot push backward against the earth.

To experience the third law of motion for yourself, you and a friend can put on your ice skates or roller skates. Stand behind your friend while you are both at rest. Place your hands on your friend's back and tell him or her that you are going to push forward. Your friend, of course, accelerates forward because of your push. What happens to you?

Repeat the experiment, but have your friend push on you. What happens this time? What happens if instead of pushing on a friend, you push against the boards around a hockey or roller-skating rink, a post beside a frozen pond, or some other object that is fixed firmly to the earth? Is your acceleration related to how hard you push?

A SPRINTER'S START

When sprinters line up for a race, they're in a crouched position with their feet against starting blocks. Sprinters who try to start from a standing position are sure to lose unless the competition is much slower than they are.

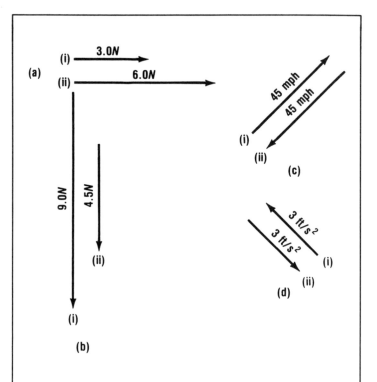

Figure 3. Vectors (arrows) can be used to represent quantities that have a magnitude (size) and a direction. The length of the arrow gives the magnitude. The head of the arrow gives the direction. (a) Vector (i) represents a horizontal force to the right of 3.0 N. Vector (ii) represents a horizontal force to the right of 6.0 N. (b) Vector (i) represents a weight of 9.0 N. Vector (ii) represents a weight of 4.5 N. (c) Vector (i) represents a velocity of 45 mph N.E. Vector (ii) represents a velocity of 45 mph S.W. (d) Vector (i) represents an acceleration of 3 ft/s^2 N.W. Vector (ii) represents an acceleration of 3 ft/s^2 S.E.

How do starting blocks help sprinters obtain a greater forward acceleration?

You can check this by having several friends who run at about the same speed run several short races of about 10 to 20 yards. Have half of them start from an upright position and the other half from a typical sprinter's position. In a second race, have those who started from an upright position start from a sprinter's start and vice versa. What evidence do you have to support the idea that a crouched position gives a sprinter an advantage over a competitor who starts from an upright position?

An explanation of why starting a race from a crouched position gives one an advantage is best developed through the use of vectors. Vectors, which are usually depicted by arrows, as shown in Figure 3, can be used to represent anything that has a magnitude and a direction. A force, for example, can be represented by a vector. You can tie a string around a roller skate and pull it. The harder you pull, the bigger the force you exert on the skate and the larger its acceleration will be. A small force can be represented by a short vector (arrow). A larger force can be represented by a longer arrow (Figure 3). The direction in which you pull the skate makes a difference, too. If you pull forward, the skate will accelerate forward. If you pull backward, the skate will accelerate in that direction. Pulling upward with a force greater than the skate's weight will cause it to accelerate upward.

Have a friend sit in a wagon that is at rest on a smooth, level surface. The wagon and your friend represent a sprinter. If possible, have your friend hold an accelerometer. An accelerometer, like the one shown in Figure 4a, will allow you to at least compare the accelerations produced by different forces. Attach a strong spring

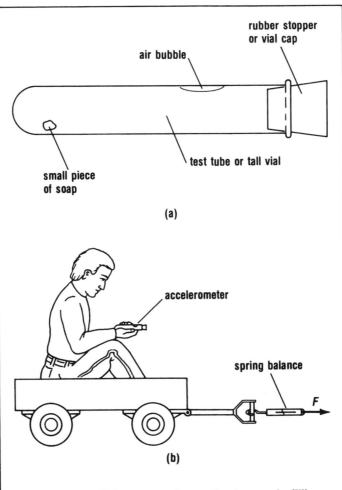

rubber stopper
or vial cap

air bubble

small piece
of soap

test tube or tall vial

(a)

accelerometer

spring balance

F

(b)

Figure 4. (a) Make an accelerometer by nearly filling a test tube or tall vial with water. Add a small piece of soap to reduce surface tension. Stopper the tube or vial. Hold the tube so the bubble can move horizontally. The small air bubble trapped in the tube will always move in the direction of any acceleration. Try it! (b) A friend sits in a wagon holding the accelerometer while you pull with a constant force.

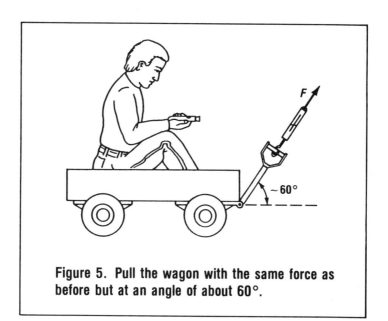

Figure 5. Pull the wagon with the same force as before but at an angle of about 60°.

balance to the wagon's handle. How much force do you have to exert to overcome friction and make the wagon move slowly forward? Now pull the wagon forward with a constant force that causes the wagon to clearly accelerate. (Figure 4*b*.) To keep a constant force on the wagon, you will have to keep the spring scale stretched by a fixed amount, and you will have to move faster and faster ahead of the wagon to do so. Your friend can make a qualitative estimate of the acceleration from the forward movement of the bubble in the accelerometer.

Now apply the same force in an upward direction. As you can see, the wagon doesn't accelerate at all. There is no force in the forward direction. Now, using the same force as before, pull forward at an angle of about 60° above the horizontal as shown in Figure 5. Then pull with the same force at about 45°, 30°, and finally straight ahead (0°). Which direction gives the greatest forward acceleration? What happens to the wagon's acceleration if you increase the force in this direction?

Using what you have learned, why does a sprinter crouch at the start of a race? Why does he or she use starting blocks?

QUESTIONS FOR FURTHER RESEARCH

- Show how velocity vectors can be used to explain why an outfielder should throw a ball horizontally, rather than at an angle upward from the horizontal.
- Where else can vectors be used to help explain the science in sports?

RUNNING THE BASES

James "Cool Papa" Bell, one of the great black baseball players who played in the Negro Leagues during the 1930s and 1940s when discrimination barred blacks from the major leagues, could circle the bases in about 13.0 seconds. It was reported that Jesse Owens, the Olympic gold medalist who won the 100-meter (109 yd) dash in 1936 with a time of 10.3 s, refused to race Bell. If Bell could run 360 feet (4 × 90 feet) or 120 yards in 13 s, his average speed was 9.23 yd/s. Owens' speed over 109 yards was 10.6 yd/s (109 yd/10.3 s). Since Owens' speed was more than a yard per second faster than Bell, why should he fear losing to Bell in a race?

You can answer this puzzle by timing a friend who rounds the bases as fast as he or she can. Then, a few minutes later, time the

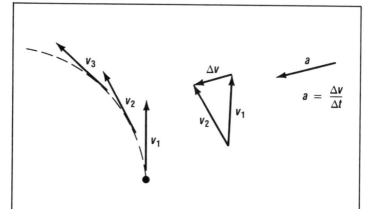

$$a = \frac{\Delta v}{\Delta t}$$

Figure 6. To move along a circular path, there must be a force perpendicular to the motion to produce a force and an acceleration that changes the direction of the velocity. The velocity change Δv is the velocity vector that must be added to v_1 to obtain the later velocity v_2. The acceleration, a, represented by a vector, is equal to $\Delta v / \Delta t$ where Δt is very small.

same person over a 120-yard dash that is along a straight line. How do the times compare? How do the speeds compare?

Why was your friend's speed on the base paths slower than along a straight line? There are several reasons. If you watch any good base runner, you'll see that he or she does not, in fact, cannot, run a straight-line path from one base to the next. Watch once more as your friend rounds the bases. Then, as closely as you can, measure the actual distance that he or she ran. How does the distance a base runner actually travels compare with the 360 feet of base paths? If you take into account the *total* distance your friend ran, what was his or her actual speed in running the bases?

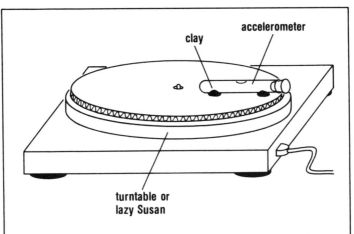

clay   accelerometer

turntable or
lazy Susan

Figure 7. An accelerometer mounted on a turntable or
lazy Susan will allow you to see the direction of the
acceleration and force on a body moving along a
circular path.

Another factor that affects a base runner's speed is
his or her need to change direction. As you know from
Newton's first law of motion, a body will continue to
move with constant velocity unless acted upon by an
outside force. (Since velocity is a vector quantity, it
involves a direction as well as a speed.) For a runner to
change direction, there must be a change in velocity.
To have a change in velocity, there must be an acceleration. To have an acceleration, there must be a force.
A base runner pushes backward against the earth to
obtain a force that pushes him or her forward. To round
a base, the runner obtains an inward force, toward the
center of the diamond, by pushing outward against the

earth. Just watch a runner who is making the turn from first to second or third to home. Notice how he or she leans inward in order to push outward against the earth. This inward (centripetal) force provides the inward acceleration that allows the runner to change direction and velocity as shown in Figure 6. Why do you think a base runner's speed would be slower while rounding a base than while running straight down the first base line in an attempt to beat out a bunt?

A simple experiment will reveal that there is an inward acceleration on a body that is moving along a curved path. Take an accelerometer and fasten it to a lazy Susan or turntable with some clay as shown in Figure 7. Give the lazy Susan a gentle push so that it spins slowly. How can you tell that there is an inward acceleration? What happens to the acceleration as the lazy Susan spins faster?

QUESTIONS FOR FURTHER RESEARCH

- On the basis of what you know about the laws of motion and vectors and your own observations of a runner rounding a base, use a stopwatch and measuring tape to make an estimate of the inward force that a base runner must develop as he or she makes a turn on the base paths.
- Find a way to measure the speed of a base runner rounding a base. Compare it to the same base runner's speed along the first base path as he or she tries to beat out a bunt.
- Why do most players not slide into first base? Why do they slide into other bases? Before a rule

change in 1870, a player who overran first base could be tagged out. Do you think players were more prone to slide into first base before 1870?

- Should a base runner attempting to steal second base take his or her first step with the right foot or the left foot? That is, should he or she start by crossing left leg over right with the push off coming from the right foot or by stepping toward second with the right foot (the one closest to second)? Design an experiment to answer this question. Then watch leading base stealers in the major leagues. With which foot do they start their move to second?

LOSING WEIGHT ON SKIS

In order to make it easier to turn their skis, skiers often engage in what they call *unweighting*. Just before they turn their skis, they may raise their bodies. If you stop to think about it, this makes a lot of sense. Raising the body is like the beginning of a jump; it takes weight off the skis.

One experiment that you can easily carry out will convince you that a skier's unweighting technique really works. Stand on a set of bathroom scales that has a dial (digital scales won't work) with your knees bent. As you watch the scale, straighten your legs. What happens to your weight?

Skiers claim that they can also reduce the weight on their skis by lowering their bodies. They say that as the upper body drops, its downward acceleration approaches that of a freely falling body and, therefore, exerts less force on the skis. Again, an experiment

By leaning, so that her skis push outward,
this skier obtains the inward (centripetal)
force needed to make a turn.

can provide the answer. Stand upright on the same set of bathroom scales, but this time watch the scale as you bend your knees. Does your weight decrease as skiers claim?

To see that the force exerted in a spring by a freely falling body is zero, hang a weight from a spring balance. Be sure that there are some thick pillows below the weight before you release the spring. Watch the dial on the spring scale closely as it falls. What force does the weight exert on the spring scale as it falls?

Repeat the experiment on the scale from the bent-knee position, but this time watch the scale closely at the very beginning. What happens to your weight at the moment you first begin to stand erect? What causes this apparent increase in weight?

WIND RESISTANCE

If you've watched speed skiers during a race, you know that they assume an almost egglike shape as they plow through the air in their slick tight-fitting outfits with arrow-shaped helmets. Cyclists, too, try to present as little of their bodies as possible to the onrushing air. In fact, cyclists in a racing team take turns serving as lead cyclist. The leader has to expend more energy to overcome air resistance so that those who follow are shielded and use less energy. By taking turns, the leader can work harder than the others for a short time and then move to the end of the line to recover while another takes on the challenge of pushing the air aside. You can see how body position affects motion through air by performing an experiment with your bicycle.

You'll need a bicycle with a speedometer, your biking helmet, a calm day (no wind), and a long stretch of level, paved road with no traffic. Make two marks on the pavement a hundred or more meters or yards apart. Pedal your bicycle as you approach the first mark so that you attain a steady speed of, say, 20 mph (32 kph) just before you reach the mark. When you reach the mark, stop pedaling and sit upright on your bicycle. Maintain that position until you reach the second mark. As you pass the second mark, read the speedometer. How much did your speed decrease?

Repeat the experiment. Be sure you have the same speed that you had before as you pass the first mark. But this time bend over so that your head and shoulders are almost in line with your buttocks. Again, read the speedometer as you pass the second mark. How does your body position affect the retarding force of the air?

What additional information do you need to determine the average deceleration for each run? What additional information do you need to determine the average force exerted by the air in each run? What is the average acceleration during each run? The average force acting during each run?

Repeat the experiments you've just performed starting at different initial speeds. How does your initial speed affect air resistance?

QUESTIONS FOR FURTHER RESEARCH

- Part of the reason for the deceleration (decreasing velocity) of your coasting bicycle is the friction between the tires and the road. With your tires at the recommended pressure and then at half that pressure measure the decrease in speed over the measured course you have laid out. What effect does the reduced pressure have on the deceleration? What should be true of your body position during this experiment?

• How can you determine your speed at different times after you have crossed the mark at which you start to slow down? How can you use that information to determine your acceleration at different times in a run? Does the acceleration change as you slow down?

• Use the values of your acceleration at different times and speeds to find out how the retarding force is affected by your velocity. Does the retarding force appear to be proportional to your velocity? Does it appear to be proportional to the square of the velocity?

• On a windy day, how much does the wind affect your motion when you coast against the wind? When you coast with the wind at your back?

3

MOMENTUM, ENERGY AND SPORTS: JUMPS, HITS, CATCHES AND THROWS

Sports fact: The center of gravity of a successful high jumper's body passes *under* the crossbar.

You've seen that a force is necessary to make a body move or change its direction of motion. The product of a force and the distance through which the force acts on a body in the direction of or against its motion is defined as the work done on the body. This work appears as an increase or a decrease in the body's energy of motion (kinetic energy). If the force increases the body's velocity,

Can you explain why a high jumper's center
of gravity must pass *below* the bar?

the kinetic energy increases; if the force acts against the motion, it reduces the kinetic energy.

The product of force and the time that the force acts is defined as the impulse applied to a body. An impulse may increase or decrease a body's momentum. Momentum is the product of a body's mass and velocity (mv).

UNWEIGHTING TECHNIQUES, IMPULSE, JUMPING, AND CATCHING

The unweighting techniques used by skiers are applied by any athlete who has to jump. At the end of a jump, just as the athlete's feet touch the ground, you'll see the jumper bend his or her knees. Usually, the jumper will also touch the ground or floor with the toes first and then roll onto the heels. Here, the purpose of bending the knees and rolling along the foot is to reduce the force needed in stopping the body.

Acceleration, as you know, is the change in an object's velocity divided by the time interval during which the velocity change takes place. This may be expressed as

$$a = \frac{\Delta V}{\Delta t}.$$

Since $F = ma$, Newton's second law can be written as

$$F = m\frac{\Delta V}{\Delta t} \quad \text{or as} \quad F\Delta t = m\Delta V.$$

The expression $F\Delta t$ is the impulse applied to a body. The expression $m\Delta v$, which is the product of the mass of an object and the change in its velocity, is the object's *change in momentum*. Its momentum, as you know, is simply *mv*. Thus, a body at rest has no momentum. If an impulse accelerates a 1-kg mass to a velocity of 10 m/s, its momentum and its change in momentum are both 10 kg-m/s. If a second impulse raises the velocity of the same mass to 25 m/s, its momentum is now 25 kg-m/s; the change in momentum brought about by the second impulse is 15 kg-m/s (25 kg-m/s − 10 kg-m/s).

The impulse that sets a body into motion and gives it momentum can also be used to stop a body that is moving and remove its momentum. This is just what happens when a jumper strikes the ground. The impulse exerted by the earth on the jumper brings him or her to rest. The impulse vector has to be equal in magnitude and opposite in direction to the momentum vector. However, the impulse may consist of a large force exerted for a short time or a small force exerted for a long time. As long as the product of the force and the time equals the momentum of the jumper and opposes his or her motion, the jumper will stop.

If you ran on pillows in the experiment described in Chapter 1, you know that although a large Δt may reduce the force on your legs, it can become so great that it reduces your speed significantly. On the other hand, a hard track brings your feet to a stop so quickly that the force on your muscles and bones may be large enough to produce soreness and tissue damage.

A simple experiment will reveal how the time in bringing your own body to rest affects the force. Stand on the first stair of a stairway and jump back to the floor so that you land with your feet flat and your legs stiff. You'll feel a fairly strong jolt in your legs. Now repeat the experiment, but this time land on your toes and bend your knees as you hit the floor. It takes longer for your body to come to a complete stop this way, but how does it feel? Why is the force that you feel less intense than the force you felt when you jumped with stiff legs and landed flat-footed?

Here's another experiment that shows how differences in the time involved in an impulse can affect the force associated with the same impulse. Put on a baseball glove and ask a friend to throw you a fairly slow pitch. Not a fast ball, please! Keep your hand stiff (don't "give") as the ball strikes the glove. Now repeat the experiment, but this time let your hand go with the pitch so that the glove moves with the ball for a short distance as you bring it to rest. Assuming the ball had the same speed in both cases, how did the two impulses that you applied to the ball compare? In which case did it take less time to bring the ball to a stop? In which case did you apply a smaller force?

How is the phrase "soft hands," which is so often heard in sports, related to the impulse involved in bringing a ball to rest? What other sports-related activities involve impulses in which the time factor in the impulse can be changed so as to change the force needed?

Try kicking a soccer ball in two different ways. First, kick the ball in such a way that your foot stops as soon as you make contact with the ball. Next, kick the ball with a "follow through" so that your foot stays in contact with the ball for as long as possible. In which case did you apply a greater impulse to the ball? In which case did the ball travel farther? Faster? In what other sports-related activities does "follow through" (the application of a larger impulse) play a role?

WORK, KINETIC ENERGY, IMPULSE, MOMENTUM, AND SPORTS

In the previous section you saw that a larger impulse, $F\Delta t$, produced by the bigger Δt associated with good follow through, produced a greater momentum change, that is, a greater $m\Delta v$. After all, the mass of the ball is constant, and since $F\Delta t = m\Delta v$, it follows that an increase in the impulse will provide a ball initially at rest with a greater velocity.

We might look at the kicking, throwing, or hitting of a ball in a different way. Instead of considering the time that a force is applied, we might look at the distance over which a force is applied. As you might expect, applying a force to a ball over a greater distance gives the ball a greater velocity change, just as applying a force for a greater time does. However, there is a difference. As you can see from Figure 8, the area under a velocity vs. time graph gives the distance traveled. If an object starting from rest accelerates uniformly, as it will under a constant force, the distance it travels, that is, the area under its velocity vs. time graph is $\frac{1}{2} vt$.

If the force applied to a body is multiplied by the distance through which the force acts in the direction of the motion, the product is defined as the work done on the body.

$$\text{Work} = \text{force} \times \text{distance} \quad \text{or } W = Fd.$$

Now if we substitute for d its equivalent, $\frac{1}{2} vt$, and for F the quantity ma then we may write:

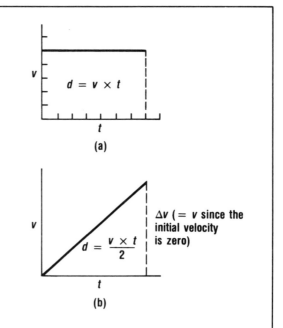

Figure 8. (a) The area under a velocity vs. time graph gives the distance traveled. (b) For body that accelerates uniformly from rest, the area under the velocity vs. time graph gives the distance. Since the area is a triangle, $d = \dfrac{1}{2}$ base × altitude $= \dfrac{1}{2}$ vt.

$$W = Fd = (ma)(\tfrac{1}{2}vt).$$

We know that for any body undergoing acceleration $a = \Delta v / \Delta t$, and, for a body starting from rest, $\Delta v = v$ and $\Delta t = t$; therefore, for such an object, $a = v / t$. Consequently, the work done can be expressed as

$$W = Fd = (ma)\left(\frac{1}{2}vt\right) = \left(m\frac{v}{t}\right)\left(\frac{1}{2}vt\right) = \frac{1}{2}mv^2.$$

In the equation above, $1/2\ mv^2$ is defined as the kinetic energy of the moving body. To acquire kinetic energy, work must be done. Of course, if some of the work done is used to overcome friction, only the net force—the force applied less the force used to overcome friction—contributes to the kinetic energy of the moving body.

In catching a baseball or kicking a soccer ball, an impulse is applied and work is done. An impulse applied to a body can lead to a gain or loss of momentum; the work done can add to, or reduce, a body's kinetic energy. A ball thrown upward into the air loses kinetic energy. Since energy is conserved, we know the energy is not lost. It simply changes from kinetic to gravitational potential energy. On the way down, the potential energy is converted back to kinetic energy. In fact, if the ball is thrown straight up, the height to which it ascends can be used to measure the work done on the ball. Since the product of the ball's weight, mg, and the height, h, to which it rises equals the work that gravity does on the ball as it rises, an equal amount of work must have been done on the ball before it was released. If the ball is thrown straight upward, the work done on the ball before its release equals the kinetic energy of the ball immediately after its release, which, in turn, equals the potential energy of the ball at the peak of its rise. Consequently, we may write:

$$F_{(avg)} \times d = \tfrac{1}{2}mv^2 = mgh.$$

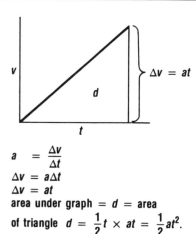

$$a = \frac{\Delta v}{\Delta t}$$
$$\Delta v = a\Delta t$$
$$\Delta v = at$$
area under graph = d = area
of triangle $d = \frac{1}{2}t \times at = \frac{1}{2}at^2.$

Figure 9. The area under a *v* vs. *t* graph is the distance traveled. Since $a = \frac{\Delta v}{\Delta t}$ **,** $\Delta v = $ $a\Delta$ ($\Delta v = a\Delta t$)*t*. **Because the motion started at** *t* = **0,** $\Delta t = t$ **and, therefore,** $\Delta v = at$. **The triangular area under the graph, the distance traveled, is equal to** $\frac{1}{2}$ **base × altitude or d** $= \frac{1}{2}t \times at = \frac{1}{2}at^2$.

WORK, ENERGY, AND TIME IN THROWING A BASEBALL

When you throw a baseball, you exert a force on the ball through some distance. You therefore do work on the ball and give it kinetic energy. How large a force do you exert when you throw a baseball? How much work is done in throwing the ball? How long does it take to make the throw? How fast does the ball move? Experiments can provide answers to these questions.

You can begin by doing an experiment that will give reasonably good estimates for answers to the questions raised above. Later, you may want to do another experiment that may give somewhat better estimates. The kinetic energy of a ball can be calculated if you know its mass and its velocity. It's easy enough to find the mass of a baseball. All you need is a balance. According to the rules, its mass should be between 142 g and 149 g (5–5.25 oz). You can make a reasonable estimate of its velocity by having a "pitcher," who has warmed up thoroughly, throw the ball horizontally on a level field. Watch the pitcher and make an estimate of the point at which he or she releases the ball. Watch also to see that the ball's initial path is very nearly horizontal. The thrower's height and point of release will help you to estimate the height of the ball above the ground when it leaves the pitcher's hand.

Once you know the ball's release height, you can determine how long the ball stays in the air. As you learned in Chapter 2, the force of gravity causes all objects near the earth's surface to fall with the same acceleration—9.8 m/s^2. This vertical acceleration holds true whether or not there is a horizontal velocity. Horizontal and vertical motions act independently of each other. The relationship between the acceleration (a) and the distance (d) that a ball travels over a time (t) is given by

$$d = \frac{1}{2} at^2.$$

The derivation for this relationship is found in Figure 9. In this experiment, the acceleration is g, 9.8 m/s^2, and d is the estimate of the height that the ball falls (its release height).

Suppose the ball is released from a height of 1.8 m (6 ft); the time for it to reach the ground can be calculated. Since $d = \frac{1}{2}at^2$, we can find the time because we know d and g:

$$t^2 = \frac{2d}{g} \quad \text{and so} \quad t = \sqrt{\frac{2 \times 1.8 \text{ m}}{9.8 \text{ m/s}^2}} = 0.61 \text{ s}.$$

If you measure the horizontal distance the ball traveled, you can find its average horizontal velocity (v_H). Suppose, for example, that the ball lands 20 m beyond the point it was released. It traveled this distance in 0.61 s; therefore, its horizontal velocity was 33 m/s:

$$v_H = \frac{20 \text{ m}}{0.61 \text{ s}} = 33 \text{ m/s or } 108 \text{ ft/s (73 mph)}.$$

The kinetic energy of the ball, which is also the work done on the ball by the pitcher, was 80 joules since

$$\tfrac{1}{2} mv^2 = 0.5 \times 0.147 \text{ kg} \times (33 \text{ m/s})^2 = 80 \text{ J}.$$

What was the horizontal velocity of the ball *your* pitcher threw? What was its kinetic energy?

To find the average force the pitcher exerts on the ball, you need to know the distance the pitcher's arm moved in throwing the ball. You can do this by having one person sight and mark the farthest backward extension of the pitcher's hand while another person sights and marks the pitcher's hand at the point the ball is released. The distance between these two points is approximately the distance through which the pitcher exerted a force on the ball. Since you know the work that was done on the ball and the distance through which the force acted, you can calculate the average force exerted on the ball.

In the example given above, if the pitcher's hand moved 2.5 m, then the average force on the ball was 32 N (7 lb) because

$$F \times d = \text{work} = \tfrac{1}{2} mv^2 = 80 \text{ J}. \quad \text{Therefore,}$$

$$F = \frac{80 \text{ J}}{d} = \frac{80\text{J}}{2.5 \text{ m}} = 32 \text{ N}.$$

Since the impulse that acted on the ball equals the momentum that the ball acquired, you can calculate the time it took the pitcher to throw the ball. Using the example above

$$F\Delta t = mv, \ \Delta t = \frac{mv}{F} = \frac{0.145 \text{ kg} \times 33 \text{ m/s}}{32 \text{ N}} = 0.15 \text{ s}.$$

What average force did your pitcher exert on the ball? How long did it take him or her to throw the ball? What force do you and other pitchers exert on the ball? How much time is spent exerting force on the ball when the ball is thrown?

THE ENERGY AND MOMENTUM OF A BATTED BALL

You can also determine the kinetic energy and momentum of a batted fly ball or one hit with a fungo bat. Because you'll need a stopwatch to measure the time the ball is in the air, the fungo bat experiment is easier to do. You can generally count on the coach (or player) to deliver a fly ball with a fungo bat. A batter may cause you to make a lot of false starts with the watch because of grounders, strikes, and pitches that are taken.

To find the kinetic energy of a batted ball you will need to know both its horizontal velocity (v_H) and its vertical velocity (v_V) at the time you hit it. Once these are known, the kinetic energy (E_K) can be determined because, as you can see from Figure 10,

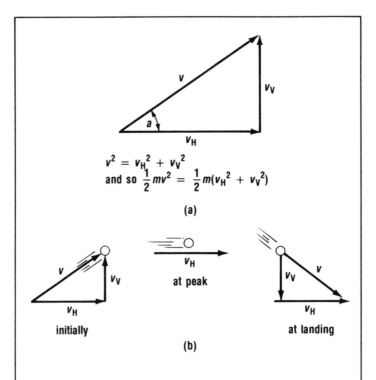

$$v^2 = v_H{}^2 + v_V{}^2$$

and so $\frac{1}{2}mv^2 = \frac{1}{2}m(v_H{}^2 + v_V{}^2)$

(a)

at peak

initially

at landing

(b)

Figure 10. (a) From the Pythagorean theorem we know that the sum of the squares of the sides of a right triangle are equal to the hypotenuse squared. In this case, the sum of the squares of the vectors representing the initial horizontal and vertical velocities of the ball equal the square of the ball's actual velocity, which is directed upward at an angle *a*. (b) After a ball is thrown or batted upward at some angle, it has a velocity, v_H, in the horizontal direction and a velocity, v_V, in the vertical direction. The vertical velocity gradually decreases until the ball reaches the peak of its flight, when it becomes momentarily zero. It then increases in the downward direction until the ball lands. The horizontal velocity remains constant throughout the flight.

$$E_K = \tfrac{1}{2} mv^2 = \tfrac{1}{2} m \,(v_H{}^2 + v_V{}^2).$$

Once the ball is hit, its horizontal velocity remains constant because the only force on the ball is gravity, which acts vertically.

Use a stopwatch to determine the total time (t) the ball is in the air. By measuring the distance (d_H) it travels horizontally, you can calculate its horizontal velocity because $v_H = d_{H/t}$.

Since all objects near the earth's surface accelerate downward at 9.8 m/s^2 the ball's initial vertical velocity can be calculated. The time for the ball to reach its peak height (where its vertical velocity will momentarily be zero) will be the time it takes for the ball's vertical velocity to change from v_V to zero. Since acceleration is the change in velocity (Δv) divided by the time (t) required to make the change,

$$\frac{\Delta v}{t} = g \quad \text{or} \quad \frac{(v_V - 0)}{t} = g \quad \text{and so} \quad v_V = gt.$$

The time for the ball to reach the peak of its path will be half its total time in the air; therefore, you can determine the ball's vertical velocity by multiplying half the ball's time in the air by g.

What was the velocity, v, of the ball when it left the bat? What was the kinetic energy of the batted ball? How much work was done on the ball?

What was the ball's momentum when it left the bat? Careful studies indicate that the ball is probably in contact with the bat for no more than one millisecond (0.001 s). Using a millisecond as the contact time, what was the average force applied to the ball by the bat?

At the top of its flight, a batted ball, while retaining its horizontal velocity, has lost all its vertical velocity. It must, therefore, have transferred some of its kinetic energy and some of its momentum. Since energy and momentum are both conserved (none of either is ever lost), what happened to the "missing" kinetic energy? What happened to the "missing" momentum? (Hint: remember the momentum of an object can change if an impulse ($F\Delta t$) causes it to exchange momentum with another body. What body exerts a force on the batted ball during the time it ascends to its peak? A body acquires kinetic energy when work is done on it. Might it lose kinetic energy if work is done against its motion?)

By the time the batted ball approaches the ground, it has regained its "missing" kinetic energy and a new momentum. How did it regain this energy and momentum?

What simplifying assumptions have you made in this experiment?

QUESTIONS FOR FURTHER RESEARCH

• To make a more accurate measurement of the force and time involved in throwing a baseball, have a pitcher throw the ball upward at an angle instead of horizontally. Use the same methods you used to find the kinetic energy and momentum of a batted ball and a thrown ball to find the average force exerted on the ball. Then, once you know the ball's momentum, find the small time interval required to make the throw.

• Measure the kinetic energy of a ball thrown by an outfielder. What is the average force the fielder exerts on the ball and through what distance does he or she exert the force? How long does it take to make the throw? Why are outfielders told to throw the ball on a line (horizontally) and make it hop rather than throw the ball in an arc that will reach the receiving player in the air?

- Why do good home-run hitters prefer to hit a fast ball?
- Using techniques similar to the ones you used for a batted baseball and thrown baseball, determine the kinetic energy of a lacrosse ball thrown a long distance by a player. What was the average force exerted on the ball and through what distance did the force act? How long did the throwing action take? Does it make a difference whether a long or a short stick is used to make the throw?
- The time that a tennis ball is in contact with the racket during a stroke is about five milliseconds (0.005 s). Design an experiment to determine the average force a tennis player applies to a ball during a stroke.

IMPULSE, ENERGY, AND THE USE OF HELMETS IN SPORTS

Photographs of hockey players in the days of Gordie Howe and Bobby Orr show players without helmets. Earlier photographs show that even football players did not wear helmets when the game was new. Serious head injuries in both sports led to rules requiring players to wear helmets. Anyone participating in a sport in which there is the possibility of a large impulse being applied to the head in a short period of time should wear a helmet. If you ride a bicycle, you should wear a helmet. To see why, consider what would happen if you were thrown from a bicycle onto a hard surface, such as pavement or concrete. If you landed headfirst, which is often the case in bicycle accidents, your head

At one time, hockey players were not
required to wear helmets. If you've
investigated the impact of a sports
collision on the head, you'll know
why the NHL now requires *all* players
to wear helmets.

would fall through a distance of about 1.5 m (5 ft). The time to fall this distance is 0.55 seconds. The velocity of your head after this time would be 5.4 m/s (18 ft/s). The time to bring your head to rest on a hard surface would be very short, let's say 5 milliseconds (0.005 s). If your mass is 50 kg (110 pounds on a bathroom scale), your momentum would be 270 kg m/s. The average force applied to your head would be

$$F = \frac{m\Delta v}{\Delta t} = \frac{270 \text{ kg m/s}}{0.005 \text{ s}} = 54,000 \text{ N } (12,000 \text{ pounds}).$$

If the landing is soft and Δt is twice as long, the force would be half as large. However, whether the force is 6 tons or 3 tons, such a force applied to your head could have serious consequences. With a helmet, the impact time is increased significantly because the suspension and padding increase the time required to bring your head to rest.

By throwing a ball of clay you can see how a greater impact time reduces the force in an impulse. First, throw the ball of clay against a brick or concrete wall. Look at its shape after it has been brought to rest. Reform the clay into a smooth sphere. Throw it again at about the same speed as before. But this time, throw it against a bed sheet hanging from a clothesline. The flexible sheet will increase the time required to bring the ball to rest. How does the shape of the ball after this impulse compare with its shape after it collided with the wall? Why are the shapes different?

QUESTIONS FOR FURTHER RESEARCH

- Cover the hitting area of a baseball bat with foam rubber. Then ask a friend to throw you a few batting-practice pitches. How does the "rubberized" bat affect your hitting? How can you explain its effect?

• You know that if you drop an egg onto the floor, the impulse applied to the egg will break it open. If you can increase the time over which the impulse is applied, you could drop the egg without breaking it. See if you can design a "helmet" for an egg that will allow you to drop the egg repeatedly onto a hard surface without breaking it. You might like to examine the construction of a number of sports helmets before you tackle this challenge!

• Could sports helmets provide even greater safety if they were made larger? If so, why aren't they bigger?

CENTER OF GRAVITY AND SPORTS

There is a point in your body, and in every material object, where all of the body's weight can be considered to be located. Any body will be balanced if supported at that point; a force acting through that point will not cause the body to rotate. That point is called the center of gravity (COG).

The COG of a ball is located at the center of the ball. The COG of a book is located close to the book's center. If you mark on the back of a pad of paper the point where two diagonals drawn across the pad meet, you will find that you can balance the pad on your finger at that point. Your own COG probably lies along your midline, several inches below your navel.

Hang a piece of thread, with a paper clip attached to its lower end, so that it hangs along the center of a full-length mirror. Stand in front of the mirror. Close one eye and move until the image of the center of your nose lies behind the thread as you stand perfectly straight. Continue to keep your eye closed as you raise your left leg. Where is the image of your eye now? How did your body move when you lifted your left leg?

Repeat the experiment. But this time raise your right leg. How does your body move this time?

If you stand with your left side fixed firmly against a wall, you can't lift your right leg without falling. Why?

As you saw in the last experiment, when you raise your left leg, your body automatically moves so as to shift your weight to the right (unless a wall prevents you from making this adjustment). By so doing, you keep your COG over a base—your right foot. If you hadn't done this (you often didn't when you were a baby learning to walk), your COG would have been to the left of your right foot. This would have created a torque (a moment of force) causing you to rotate to your left and fall to the floor. By shifting your weight to the right, you keep your COG over your right foot so that there is no torque to cause rotation and a fall. See Figure 11.

If you water-ski, you know that you have to lean back to avoid a spill. By so doing, your weight creates a backward torque to balance the forward torque produced by the rope.

For every torque, there is an equal and opposite torque. This is the rotational equivalent of the third law of motion. It becomes evident whenever you walk.

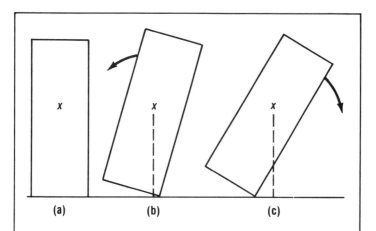

Figure 11. (a) A block is stable as long as its COG, marked here with an "x," lies over its base. (b) If the block is tipped but its COG is over its base, it will rotate back to its stable position when released. (c) If tipped until its COG is beyond its base, it becomes unstable and will fall over.

Ask a friend to stand so that his COG is in line with a weighted string hung from the ceiling. Now ask your friend to bend over and touch his toes. To do so, his head and some of his upper body will move well out in front of his COG. Watch what happens to the rest of his body. How does he compensate so as to keep his COG above his feet?

If you stand with your heels and back against a wall, you'll find that you can't reach down and touch your toes. And if you persist in your effort to do so, you'll take a fall. Why?

When you walk or run, as your right leg moves forward it creates a counterclockwise torque (from your viewpoint) about your

COG. Notice what happens to your right arm and shoulder as your right leg moves forward? What is the direction of its torque about your COG? What happens to your right arm and shoulder as your left leg moves forward?

In any sport, it's important to keep your COG over your feet. Coaches in many sports tell athletes to maintain a wide base—keep his or her feet well apart—and stay low. A player in a low, wide stance will have to be tipped or pushed through a large angle before his or her COG lies beyond the body's base (feet).

Test this for yourself. Stand upright on soft, grassy ground with your feet close together. Ask a friend to give you a gentle push sideways, just enough so that you have to move your feet so as not to lose your balance. Then repeat the experiment with your feet spread well apart with one foot slightly ahead of the other. How does the push required to make you lose your balance now compare with the earlier push?

Repeat the experiment again, but this time, before the second push is applied, go into a low, crouched position. How does the push required to make you lose your balance from the second position compare with the force needed from the previous standing position?

A QUESTION FOR FURTHER RESEARCH

• When you jump into the air for a lay-up shot, to catch a line drive, a pass from a quarterback, or on the takeoff for a high jump, you raise your COG. To see how high someone raises his or her COG during a standing jump, place two meter sticks or yardsticks end to end vertically beside a person who is standing at rest on the ground or floor. Measure the distance from the ground to the person's COG. Then have that person bend and leap as high as possible into the air. Watch the person's COG to see how far it ascends. Through what height did the person raise his or her COG?

Repeat the experiment with a number of people. What was the maximum height to which anyone raised his or her COG? What was the average height to which people raised their COGs?

Considering what you have found, how can anyone jump over a bar 7 feet (2.1 m) above the ground?

TORQUES, ANGULAR MOMENTUM, FOOTBALLS, AND FIGURE SKATERS

As you know, applying a torque to a body will make it rotate. Once a body is rotating, it has angular momentum. A body with a mass m, moving at a velocity v, has a momentum mv. The same body rotating in circular fashion about a point a distance r (for radius) away has an angular momentum equal to mvr. The formulas for angular momentum vary, but all involve the body's mass, velocity, and distance from the center of rotation.

Both momentum and angular momentum are conserved. That is, the momentum or angular momentum of a body does not change unless an impulse (in the case of momentum) or a torque (in the case of angular momentum) acts on the body. Depending on the direction of the impulse or torque, it may increase or decrease the momentum or angular momentum.

You may remember how difficult it was to maintain your balance when you were learning to ride a bicycle. If someone gave you a big push, it may have been frightening, but once you were moving at a higher speed, you found the task easier. As the bicycle wheels turned faster, they acquired more angular momentum. This meant that a larger torque was required to change the bike's path. As a result, slight shifts in your own position have less effect on the bike than they had at a slower speed.

To see the effect of a torque on a football, you can begin by throwing the ball with a force that acts through its COG. To do that, throw the ball with your hand perpendicular to the ball's axis along the fattest part of the ball. Since there is no torque, the ball is a "floater"; it doesn't rotate.

Now throw the ball by gripping the laces. As you release the ball, your fingers, which are about 10 cm (4 inches) from the ball's COG, apply a torque. The result is a spiral pass. Such a pass retains its angular momentum and moves with far less air resistance than the floater you threw first. If you watch a spiral pass in slow motion on television, conservation of angular momentum is clearly illustrated by the ball's regular rotation.

Now try punting the ball. What will happen if your foot strikes the ball so that the force acts through the ball's COG? How can you kick the ball so as to make it spiral?

Place the ball on a kicking tee. What will happen if you kick the ball so that your toe is aimed directly at the ball's COG? What happens if you kick the ball below its COG? When a team tries an onside (short) kick in an effort to recover what becomes a free ball after it has traveled ten yards, the kicker usually kicks the ball *above* its COG. How does this produce a result different from that of kicking the ball below its COG?

An onside kick often bounces quite high the third time it bounces from the ground. This means that it acquires more gravitational potential energy than it had on previous bounces. What do you think is the source of this energy? Design an experiment to test your assumption.

You have probably seen a figure skater go into a camel spin with one leg and her arms extended. Have you noticed what she does in order to increase her rate of rotation? Have you seen a diver or a gymnast rotate about his or her COG during a dive or a dismount? Notice how the athlete's rotation rate increases as her body changes from the layout position to a pike or tuck position. These changes in rotation rate are based on the principle of conservation of angular momentum.

Sit in an office chair that rotates freely—preferably one with arms since it's a lot safer. Hold a weight or a small, securely fastened bag of sand in each hand and extend your arms and legs. Ask someone to give your legs a gentle push. The torque being applied to your body makes you begin to rotate in the chair. Once you are rotating, bring the weights in your hands in to your chest and bend your legs so that your feet are closer to the axis of rotation. What happens to your rate of rotation? What happens when you again extend your arms and legs? Using the principle of conservation of angular momentum, explain why your rate of rotation increased when you moved the weights and your feet inward.

What will happen if your friend applies a push in line with your COG rather than to your extended legs? In what other sports does angular momentum play an important part?

- If you stand on the ground with your feet spread, you'll find that you can throw your arms to the right or left, leap into the air, and land facing in the opposite direction. You might think that this is an impossibility because if your upper body acquires angular momentum in one direction, your lower body should acquire an equal amount of angular momentum in the opposite direction. The key is your feet. As long as your feet are in contact with the floor, you can exert a force, produce a torque, and add angular momentum to your body.

  When you're in a swimming pool, tread water so that your body is vertical and your arms stretched out in front of you just below the water's surface. Stop all movement for a moment and then bring your arms down quickly, creating a torque around your COG. What happens to your feet? How do you explain their movement? What happens to your lower body if you rotate your arms backward under water?

- Watch a diver leaving the board. How does he or she manage to do a somersault if angular momentum is conserved? How can divers perform twists?

4

LIFTS, CURVES, AND BOUNCES: PUTTING "ENGLISH" ON THE BALL

Sports facts: The distance of 60.5 feet (18.4 m) from pitcher's mound to home plate was established in 1893. Prior to 1901, a foul ball did not count as a strike.

If you play baseball, tennis, basketball, or golf, you're familiar with the fact that a ball may do strange things if you make it spin when you throw it or hit it. The head of a golf club is angled so that when it strikes the ball it will cause it to spin as well as to move forward. (See Figure 12.) Putting English on a tennis ball or basketball can produce an abnormal bounce or rebound. Some people claim that a pitcher can make a baseball curve, drop, or rise by applying an appropriate spin to the ball as it is released.

Investigations of the effect of spin on a ball were conducted long before baseball was played. Sir Isaac Newton, perhaps the greatest scientist and mathematician who ever lived, was well aware of the science in sports. In 1671, he wrote about an effect he had observed in tennis, an effect that is particularly appropriate for this chapter. "I remembered that I had often seen a tennis ball struck with an oblique racket describe (follow) . . . a curved line. For a circular (spin) as well as a progressive (forward) motion being communicated to it by that stroke, its parts on that side where the motions conspire must press and beat the contiguous air more violently, and there excite a reluctancy and reaction of the air proportionately greater."

What Newton is saying is that the ball spinning in air creates a force that is greater on one side of the sphere than on the other. Such a force was later given a name—the Magnus force. J. J. Thomson, the man who discovered the electron, was taken by the fact that the Magnus force was very similar to a force he had discovered when he passed a beam of electrons through a magnetic field perpendicular to the beam.

THOMSON, MAGNUS, AND SPINNING GOLF BALLS

In 1910, J. J. Thomson delivered a lecture describing experiments designed to discover the effect of spin on

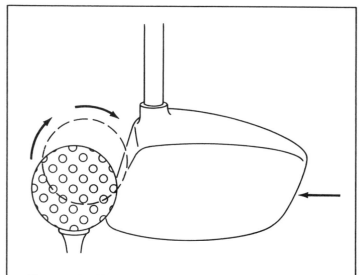

Figure 12. The angled head of a golf club causes the ball to be set into rotation with a backspin as it is driven forward.

golf balls. The first experiment he described was one performed by Gustav Magnus in 1852. Magnus placed a cylinder that could be made to spin at one end of a long rod suspended from a thread as shown in Figure 13*a*. If a stream of air flowed by the cylinder while it was spinning, the rod would be deflected as shown in Figure 13*b*. Magnus discovered that the force on the cylinder was always in the direction that the nose of the cylinder (the side of the cylinder closest to the wind) was moving.

He reasoned that a similar force should exist on a spinning ball thrown in still air. After all, the ball had

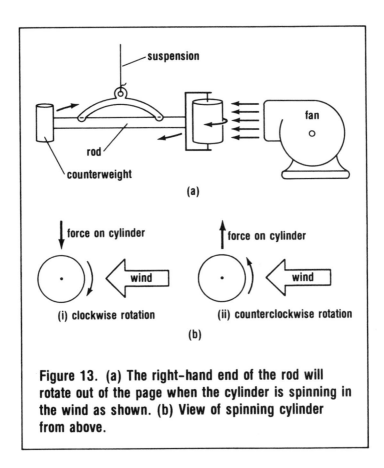

Figure 13. (a) The right-hand end of the rod will rotate out of the page when the cylinder is spinning in the wind as shown. (b) View of spinning cylinder from above.

no way of knowing whether it was moving into the air or the air was moving into it.

You can check to see if Magnus was right about the force on a spinning ball by doing an experiment in a large room where there is enough space to throw a ball. To avoid breaking anything, you can use a Styrofoam ball, like the ones used as "snowballs" in

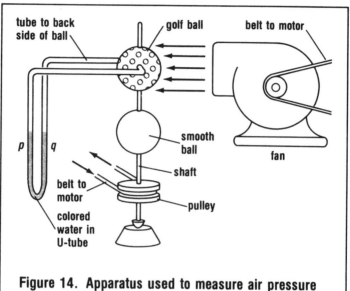

Figure 14. Apparatus used to measure air pressure on opposite sides of a golf ball. The ball can be left motionless or rotated by means of a motor connected to a pulley as shown. Another motor is used to turn a fan and generate an air stream (wind).

decorating Christmas trees. If you can't find such a Styrofoam ball, use a beach ball. Hold the ball in both hands. As you push it forward, use one hand to apply a clockwise or counterclockwise spin to the ball as it leaves your hands. If you're an experienced baseball player, you can probably apply the spin by turning your wrist as you release the ball. Watch the ball closely after you release it. Of course, it will fall because of gravity, but does it also curve to the right or left? Remember Magnus's rule—the force on the ball will be in the direction that the nose of the ball is moving as it moves into the wind. (See Figure 13*b*).

Repeat the experiment, but this time spin the ball in the opposite direction. Is the force now in the opposite direction as Magnus's rule predicts?

QUESTION FOR FURTHER RESEARCH

- Design an experiment similar to the one Magnus did. You'll probably need a fan that can generate a strong wind. In place of the cylinder, you might use a ball suspended from a thread. By winding the thread, you can make the ball spin in either direction. Of course, the ball will also be pushed backward by the wind. How can you determine whether it is also being pushed sideways? What can you do to measure the actual force on the ball?

By rotating a golf ball in an air stream, Thomson was able to show that the pressure on one side of the ball is greater than on the other side. He used an apparatus like the one shown in Figure 14. The golf ball was attached to a shaft with a pulley at the lower end. A motor connected to the pulley by a belt was used to rotate the golf ball. A strong fan driven by another motor was used to create an air stream (wind) across the ball. A U-shaped pressure gauge containing colored water was used to measure the air pressure on opposite sides of the ball. If the liquid rose higher in one side of the tube, say p, than in the other, q, then the air beside the ball leading through a tube to p was at a pressure lower than the pressure of the air on the opposite side.

Thomson could show very clearly that:

• If the wind was blowing and the golf ball was *not* rotating, the air pressure was the same on both sides of the ball. (The liquid levels on both sides of the U-tube were at the same height.)

• If the wind was not blowing and the golf ball was spinning, the pressure was still the same on both sides of the ball.

• If the wind was blowing and the ball was spinning counterclockwise (as viewed from above in Figure 14), the air pressure on the outside of the ball (the side you can see in Figure 14) was greater than the pressure on the other side. (The liquid was higher at q than at p.)

• If the wind was blowing and the ball was spinning clockwise, the air pressure was greater on the inside of the ball than on the outside. (The liquid was higher at p than at q.)

• If the golf ball is replaced by a smooth ball, the pressure difference between the two sides of the ball is about half as large as it is with the golf ball rotating at the same rate in the same wind speed.

Do these results agree with what you found when you threw a spinning ball?

J. J. Thomson was probably intrigued by these experiments because the force on the golf ball was perpendicular to both the ball's velocity and its axis of rotation. In his experiments with electrons, Thomson had found that electrons with a velocity perpendicular to a magnetic field experienced a force that was per-

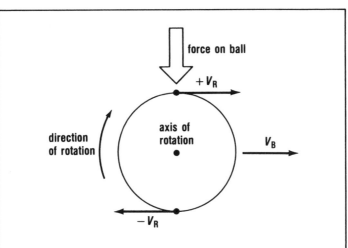

Figure 15. A ball moving through air with a velocity V_B is rotating clockwise as seen here. Each point on the circumference of the ball at its equator has a speed V_R due to rotation. However, a point at the top of the ball is moving with a velocity $V_B + V_R$; a point on the bottom of the ball is moving with a velocity $V_B - V_R$.

pendicular to both their velocity and the direction of the magnetic field.

In any case, his experiments show that for a rotating ball moving through air, the pressure is greater on the side of the ball that is moving faster; that is, the side that is turning in the same direction that the ball is moving. This phenomenon is illustrated in Figure 15 where you can see that the velocity of a point at the top of the ball is greater than the velocity of a point at the bottom of the ball. It's similar to walking on an escalator. If you walk in the direction the escalator is moving, you ascend faster than if you stand still. On the other hand, if you walk slowly *down* the escalator, you ascend at a lesser velocity than someone who simply stands on the same escalator.

A rough ball, such as a baseball with its raised stitches, a golf ball with its dimples, or a tennis ball with its fuzz carries some air forward as it spins (top of ball in Figure 15) or backward (bottom of ball in Figure 15). The air carried forward by the part of the ball that is spinning in the direction the ball is moving increases the concentration of air on that side of the ball. On the other side, the air carried away by the ball reduces the concentration of air. As a result, the air pressure is greater on the side where the concentration of air is increased (the top of the ball in Figure 15). This is what Newton meant when he wrote: ''. . . its parts on that side where the motions conspire must press and beat the contiguous air more violently, and there excite a reluctancy and reaction of the air proportionately greater.''

Suppose the difference in air pressure on the two sides of a golf ball due to its rotation is 0.3 percent of the atmospheric pressure. Air pressure at sea level is about 10 N/cm^2 (14.5 lbs/sq in). The diameter of a golf ball is about 4.28 cm (1.68 in), and its area of cross section is 14.4 cm^2 (2.2 sq in). The product of the pressure (force/area) and the area of cross section gives us the force on the ball. If the pressure on the bottom of the ball exceeds the pressure on the top by 0.3 percent, then the force lifting the ball is given by

$$0.003 \times 10 \text{ N/cm}^2 \times 14.4 \text{ cm}^2 = 0.43 \text{ N}.$$

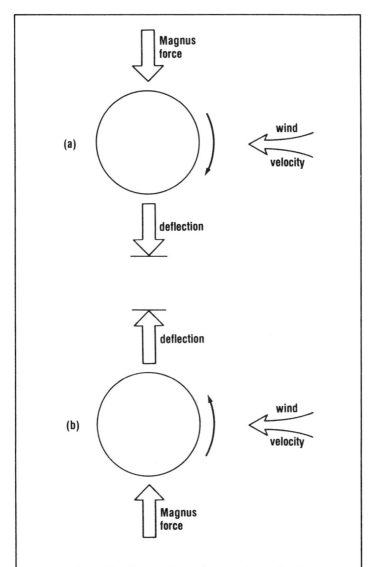

Figure 16. (a) With a clockwise rotation, the ball was deflected to the right of the oncoming wind. (b) With a counterclockwise rotation, the ball was deflected to the left of the oncoming wind.

The mass of a golf ball is about 44 grams (0.044 kg), so it weighs about 0.43 N. This means that the lift force on the golf ball in question is just about equal to its weight. At greater rates of rotation the lift force may exceed the ball's weight, which explains why the angle of ascent of a well-driven golf ball may increase after it leaves the club.

Try throwing a Styrofoam ball or a beach ball with a lot of backspin—the spin given to a well-driven golf ball. Can you make the ball ascend after it leaves your hand? What happens to the flight of the ball if you give it the opposite (top or forward) spin as it leaves your hand?

OTHER EXPERIMENTS WITH ROTATING BALLS

In 1959, Lyman J. Briggs reported the results of experiments he had performed with spinning baseballs in a wind tunnel. Briggs dropped the balls across a six-foot-wide wind tunnel after setting them in rotation about a vertical axis so that the rotation axis would be perpendicular to the air flow in the tunnel. Lampblack was spread over the ball so that its deflection relative to a vertical line of fall could be measured. The balls were made to rotate by a belt-driven spinner connected to a motor. A suction cup at the end of a rotating shaft kept the ball from falling until a valve that connected the cup to normal air pressure was opened. The ball's rate of spin was measured with a calibrated stroboscope.

Figure 16 shows the direction the ball was deflected relative to the wind velocity as viewed from above the wind tunnel. Are these deflections what you

Table 2. **The lateral deflection of a spinning baseball during a six-foot drop across a wind tunnel**[a]

Ball's rate of spin (rev/s)	Wind speed (ft/s)	(m/s)	(mph)	Deflection (in)	(m)
20	75	22.9	51	6.1	0.15
20	100	30.5	68	11.7	0.297
20	125	38.1	85	17.8	0.452
20	150	45.7	102	26.0	0.660
30	75	22.9	51	9.4	0.239
30	100	30.5	68	17.5	0.445
30	125	38.1	85	25.8	0.655

[a] (Data is from an article by Lyman J. Briggs that appeared in the *American Journal of Physics*, vol. 27, p. 591, 1959.)

would expect on the basis of the experiments you did? Of course, the ball was deflected backward as well because of the wind, but that force was perpendicular to the deflection due to the spin and so had no bearing on the deflection to the right or left of the wind velocity.

Some of Briggs's data is in Table 2. The deflection is given as one-half the distance between the ball's landing points when the ball was spinning first clockwise and then in the opposite direction. Thus, the deflection in the table is the average deflection due to spin.

The deflection of the ball is due, of course, to the Magnus force that acts on it as it falls across the wind. With a force, there will be an acceleration, and the relationship between the acceleration and the distance the ball is deflected is given by the familiar relationship $d = \frac{1}{2} at^2$, which was developed in Chapter 3.

You can use the data in Table 2 to answer some questions and draw some conclusions of your own.

- If the wind speed is kept constant at 75, 100, or 125 ft/s, perhaps the deflection is proportional to the ball's rate of spin. To find out, you can compare the ratio of spin rates to the corresponding ratio of deflections. Is the deflection proportional to the rate of spin? How do you know?
- To see how the deflection is related to the wind speed for a fixed spin rate, say 20 rev/s, you can plot a graph of deflection vs. wind speed. (Don't forget to plot the origin—zero deflection for zero spin.) Is the graph a straight line? What does this tell you?

  Next, try a graph of deflection vs. the *square* of the wind speed. What do you find? How do you know that the deflection is proportional to the square of the wind speed?
- The time for a ball to fall 6 feet (1.83 meters) is easily determined. We know that over such a short fall its vertical acceleration would be 9.8 m/s^2. The time to fall through this distance was calculated in Chapter 3 and found to be 0.61 s.

  During its fall the ball is deflected (pushed) sideways by the Magnus force. Now that you know the time required for this deflection to occur, you can calculate the ball's sideways acceleration using the familiar equation $d = \frac{1}{2} at^2$. What are these accelerations at a spin rate of 20 rev/s and wind speeds of 75, 100, 125, and 150 ft/s?

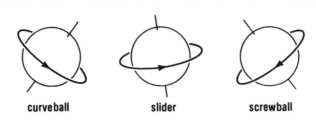

curveball　　　　**slider**　　　　**screwball**

Figure 17. Spin (as seen by a batter) of a normal curveball, slider, and screwball as thrown by a right-hand pitcher to a right-handed batter.

- The mass of a baseball is about 0.15 kg. What are the Magnus forces acting on the ball at a spin rate of 20 rev/s and wind speeds of 75, 100, 125, and 150 ft/s?

TAKING EXPERIMENTAL RESULTS TO THE FIELD OF PLAY

Whether a spinning ball is moving through still air or is at rest in a wind tunnel, air flows over the ball. A pitcher throwing a baseball, a tennis player stroking a ball with a racquet, or a basketball player making a lay-up shot can apply spin (English) to the ball. Consequently, when balls are thrown or hit so as to produce rotation, we should expect to see them deflect in the same way as spinning balls that fall vertically across air flowing through a wind tunnel.

Use a tennis racket to gently strike a Styrofoam ball in a large room or basement. As you make contact, pull the racket to the right

93

or left so as to apply a clockwise or a counterclockwise spin to the ball. Based on previous experiments, does the ball curve as you would predict in both cases?

Now try the experiment on a tennis court. How can you make your serves curve to the right? To the left? What will happen to the distance the ball travels if you apply topspin to the ball? You can do this by turning the top edge of your racket down as you stroke the ball. What happens if you apply backspin to the ball?

If you're an experienced pitcher, you probably know how to throw a curveball by turning your wrist as you release the ball. Or ask someone who is a pitcher to let you stand behind the pitcher's mound as he or she throws a curve. Then watch the same kind of pitch from behind home plate. To watch in safety, stand behind a backstop. Do you think the ball really curves?

Usually, the spin applied by a pitcher is not about a vertical axis. Rather the axis is tipped as shown in Figure 17 for a right-handed pitcher. How should such a spinning ball be deflected as it moves through air? Many pitchers can make the ball spin about a vertical axis. The resulting pitch is called a slider. Why do you think it's called a slider?

What kind of spin should a pitcher apply to make a ball drop; that is, fall faster than it normally would? If you or someone you know can throw a drop, watch what happens as that pitch approaches home plate. How does its path compare with the "meatball" pitches thrown for batting practice?

A screwball, or inshoot, is a pitch that curves the opposite way from an ordinary curveball. It curves in toward a right-hand batter when thrown by a right-hand pitcher or toward a left-hand batter when thrown by a lefty. What kind of rotation should a pitcher apply in order to throw a screwball? How can this be done? If you or someone you know can apply such rotation to a ball, watch the ball after it is thrown. Does it curve as predicted?

How does Roger Clemens of the
Boston Red Sox put the spin on
the ball? Does his hand position
in this photo reveal anything?

If you can't find someone who can throw such a pitch, you can probably do it by using a Styrofoam ball and a very gentle twist of the wrist motion. Can you throw a screwball using such a ball?

For many years, people did not believe a baseball could actually be made to curve. Then, in 1870, a pitcher in New Haven, Connecticut, named Freddy Goldsmith snapped his wrist as he released a pitch toward three vertical rods stuck in the ground along a straight line between the pitcher and his catcher. The ball went to the left of the first rod, to the right of the second, and to the left of the third showing that it did indeed follow a curved path.

Using the information above, we're ready to figure out how much a curveball is actually deflected by the Magnus force. A 68 mph (100 ft/s) curveball will take just about 0.6 seconds to reach home plate.

$$\frac{60 \text{ ft}}{100 \text{ ft/s}} = 0.60 \text{ s.}$$

This is the same time it took the ball to fall across the wind tunnel in the experiment described above. Therefore, we would expect the ball to be deflected by 11.7 inches if it's rotating at 20 rev/s or 17.5 inches at 30 rev/s. Of course, it's unlikely that the ball's spin axis will be vertical, so the horizontal deflection will probably be somewhat less.

A pitch thrown at 75 ft/s (51 mph) will require 0.8 s to reach home plate. The deflection of a ball spinning at 20 rev/s in a 75 ft/s wind was 6.1 inches in 0.6 seconds. If the ball is thrown by a pitcher, it will

Table 3. Deflections of pitches thrown at different speeds with different rotation rates

Speed (*ft/s*)	Spin (*rev/s*)	Deflection in 60 ft (*in*)
75	20	10.8
75	30	16.7
100	20	11.7
100	30	17.5
125	20	11.4
125	30	16.5
150	20	11.6

require 0.8 seconds to reach the batter. Since the deflection of the ball is proportional to the square of the time (remember $d = \frac{1}{2} at^2$), the deflection will not be 6.1 inches but 10.8 inches because

$$6.1 \text{ in} \times \left(\frac{0.8}{0.6}\right)^2 = 10.8 \text{ in.}$$

You can prove to yourself that at 125 ft/s (85 mph) only 0.48 seconds are required for the ball to reach the plate. At 150 ft/s (102 mph) it takes only 0.40 seconds. At a rotation rate of 20 rev/s, these pitches will be deflected 11.7 inches and 11.6 inches, respectively. The results for pitches at several speeds and rotations are summarized in Table 3.

As you can see, in the range of the speeds of most pitches, the deflection of the ball is proportional to the rate of spin. However, because the time for the ball to reach the plate depends on the speed at which it is thrown, the amount that the ball curves is almost independent of its speed.

Batters preparing to swing at a pitch, or tennis players receiving a serve, claim that the ball curves away sharply just before it reaches them. Golfers with a tendency to hook or slice the ball say that their drive looked straight in the beginning but curved away sharply at the end. Are these people correct, or are they just making up excuses to cover their strikes, misses, or lost golf balls?

If you did an earlier calculation, you found that a baseball thrown at 100 ft/s (30.5 m/s) with a spin of 20 rev/s is accelerated sideways at 1.6 m/s^2 (5.25 ft/s^2) by a Magnus force of 0.24 N (0.054 lb). It is this force acting on the 0.15 kg (0.33 lb) ball that causes it to curve. As you know, it takes this ball 0.60 seconds to travel the 60 feet between pitcher and batter. You can map the path of such a curveball by calculating how far it has moved and how much it has been deflected at 0.1-second intervals. In that way, you can see if the path matches that described by batters. For example, 0.4 seconds after its release the ball has traveled 12 meters toward the plate.

$$30.5 \text{ m/s} \times 0.4 \text{ s} = 12.2 \text{ m}.$$

It has been deflected sideways by 0.13 meters. Since the ball's acceleration is 1.6 m/s^2 and its deflection is given by $d = \frac{1}{2} at^2$, you can calculate how far it has been pushed sideways after 0.4 seconds.

$$d = \tfrac{1}{2} at^2 = 0.5 \times 1.6 \text{ m/s}^2 \times (0.4 \text{ s})^2 = 0.13 \text{ m } (13 \text{ cm or } 5 \text{ in}).$$

Now you can calculate the distance traveled and the deflection for 0.1, 0.2, 0.3, 0.5, and 0.6 seconds. Then make a scale drawing of the ball's path over the 18.3 m (60 ft) from the pitcher's mound to home plate. To make the curvature more apparent over such a long distance, use the length of one square on graph paper to represent each meter between pitcher and plate. Use the length of ten squares to represent one meter of deflection. The point representing the position of the ball 0.4 seconds after being thrown is given in Figure 18.

QUESTIONS FOR FURTHER RESEARCH

- If a pitcher threw a baseball at a speed of 150 ft/s and a spin rate of 30 rev/s, how much would the ball be deflected by the time it reached the batter?
- Using the data in Tables 2 and 3, how would you determine the number of times a ball rotates while it travels from pitcher to catcher?
- Use a long piece of yarn and some tape to determine the number of rotations a curveball makes in traveling from pitcher to catcher.
- If you can obtain access to a pitching machine (your local high school may have one), have a coach or someone familiar with the machine show you how it can be used to throw curveballs. If possible, use the machine to see how spin and speed cause the ball to be deflected. Use the machine first to throw straight fastballs. Once the position at which straight balls pass the plate is determined, you can begin experimenting with different spins, spin axes, and speeds. Do your experiments confirm the results found in Tables 2 and 3?
- Can the path of a bowling ball be affected by

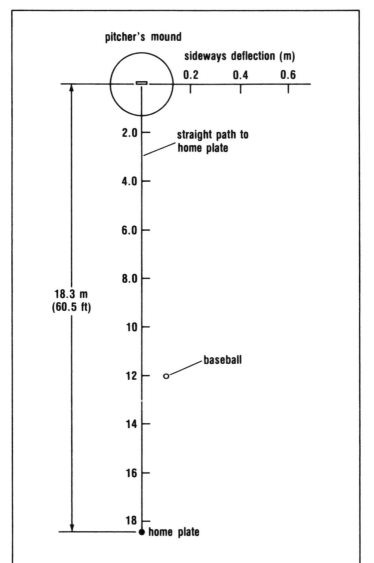

pitcher's mound

sideways deflection (m)

0.2   0.4   0.6

straight path to
home plate

2.0

4.0

6.0

8.0

18.3 m
(60.5 ft)

10

baseball

12

14

16

18

home plate

Figure 18. After 0.4 seconds, this curveball is 12 meters from the pitcher's mound and deflected 0.13 meters. Calculate the positions at other times to map the path of the pitch.

spin rate, spin axis, and speed along the alley? If so, how do these factors affect the ball's path?

SPIN, BOUNCE, AND FRICTION

You've seen that the path of a spinning ball is deflected from the path it would otherwise follow. But what happens when a spinning ball strikes a surface? Does the spin have any effect on the bounce?

Throw a Styrofoam ball as you have done before with a lot of backspin, but this time make the ball bounce as if you were throwing a bounce pass to a teammate in basketball. Compare the bounce of the ball that has a lot of backspin with the bounce of a ball thrown with very little spin. How do they compare?

See if you can predict how the ball will bounce if you throw it with a lot of top or forward spin. Were you right? How can you explain these different bounce patterns? Can you make a tennis ball bounce in the same way? How about a baseball? A basketball?

In Figure 19a, you see a diagram showing the momentum of an ideal ball that strikes the floor at an angle. The ball has no spin, and it is assumed that friction and energy losses are negligible. Part of the ball's momentum is toward the floor and part is parallel to the floor. These two parts of the ball's momentum, M, are represented by the vectors M_V and M_H, respectively. Since no horizontal force is applied to the ball, it retains its horizontal momentum. However, when the ball strikes the floor, it receives a vertical impulse that first brings it to rest (as the ball is compressed) and then pushes it back with an equal momentum as it

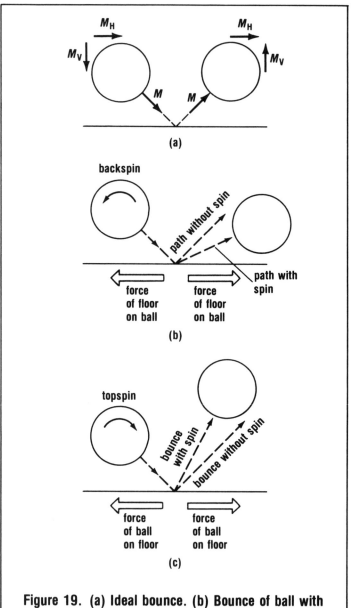

Figure 19. (a) Ideal bounce. (b) Bounce of ball with backspin. (c) Bounce of ball with topspin.

recoils back to its normal shape. As a result, the ball bounces away with the same horizontal momentum and an equal, but oppositely directed, vertical momentum.

In Figure 19*b*, the ball has backspin and there is friction between the ball and the floor. Because of the backspin, there is a forward horizontal force exerted on the floor by the ball. Based on the third law of motion, we know that the floor will provide an equal and opposite force to the ball. The resulting horizontal force pushing backward on the ball will reduce its forward speed and rate of spin, cause it to lose some kinetic energy, and thereby reduce the height of its bounce.

On the other hand, a ball with lots of topspin (Figure 19*c*) will receive a forward force from the floor that will increase its speed and kinetic energy, causing it to bounce higher than it normally would.

Can you put enough backspin on a ball so that it will actually bounce backward? Try it first with a Styrofoam ball that you let fall to the floor. Then try it with some forward motion as well as backspin. Can you do this with a tennis ball? A baseball? A lacrosse ball? A Ping-Pong ball? A handball? Can you make a backspin lob on the tennis court that will cause the ball to bounce back toward you? If you can make a topspin lob on the tennis court, what do you predict will happen when the ball lands?

In the examples shown in Figure 19, it was assumed that energy losses were negligible. To see if that's really the case when a ball bounces, let a variety of balls fall to the floor without spin from a fixed height. Do they rebound to their original height? Is any energy lost? How do you know?

To see an extreme example of energy loss, roll some modeling clay into a ball. Let this ball fall to the floor. What happens? How much kinetic energy is lost? What do you think happened to all this energy?

QUESTIONS FOR FURTHER RESEARCH

- Should a basketball player apply spin to a ball when he or she launches a shot from outside the key? If so, what kind of spin should be applied? What kind of spin is used in making a reverse lay-up? Why? Do you think it's possible to make a lay-up shot by applying spin to a ball while standing directly beneath the basket? If you do, what kind of spin do you think should be applied to the ball? Try it! Were you right?
- The origin of baseball can probably be found in a combination of two English games—rounders and cricket. In cricket, a bowler throws a ball with a stiff overhand delivery toward a batsman. Does the bowler, like a pitcher in baseball, ever apply spin to the ball? If so, what kind of spins are used and how do they affect the ball?
- In what sports other than baseball, basketball, and tennis do players apply spin to a ball? Investigate these sports to see how spin is used to give the player using it an advantage.

5

COLLISIONS IN SPORTS: BATS, BALLS, AND BOUNCES

Sports fact: A competitor in riflery is coached to squeeze the trigger between heartbeats; otherwise, a reverberation through the chest to the shoulder may send the bullet off course.

Collisions are an integral part of athletics. Not just the collision of bodies that occurs in sports like football, hockey, and lacrosse, but the collision of bat with ball, ground, or glove in baseball, the collision of ball and racket in tennis or squash, ball with floor or backboard in basketball, and even the collision of feet with court, floor, or ground that takes place in every sport.

Collisions are common and frequent in any sport.

We'll begin with the collision of ball with floor. You may not be surprised to learn that in many sports there are rules governing such collisions.

ELASTICITY OR BOUNCINESS: THE COEFFICIENT OF RESTITUTION

Collisions are classified as elastic or inelastic. An elastic collision is one in which there is no loss of kinetic energy. Elastic collisions are common in the atomic world, but the collisions we normally observe are inelastic. Some, like the collision of a ball of modeling clay with the floor, are totally inelastic. Others, like the collision of billiard balls or marbles, are almost elastic because very little kinetic energy is lost.

Tests conducted on baseballs show that balls fired at 85 ft/s at a concrete-backed ash wall rebound with an average velocity of 48 ft/s. From this information, you can determine the coefficient of restitution of a baseball.

The coefficient of restitution (COR) is defined as the ratio of the velocity with which two bodies separate after colliding to the velocity of their approach prior to colliding. Written as a formula:

$$COR = \frac{\text{velocity of separation}}{\text{velocity of approach}} \quad \text{or} \quad COR = \frac{v_2}{v_1}.$$

Since a COR of 1.0 would mean the collision involved no decrease of velocity, the collision would have to be elastic. Consequently, unless we're talking about molecular collisions, COR values are less than 1.

A simple way to measure the COR of a ball is to

Table 4. Coefficient of Restitution for Balls Used in Various Sports.

Ball	COR	Ball	COR
baseball	0.57	soccer	0.75
basketball	0.75	softball	0.55
golf ball	0.60	squash ball	0.52
handball	0.80	tennis ball	0.70

drop it from a known height, H, and then measure the height, h, to which it rebounds. The COR is the square root of the ratio of the rebound height to the height from which the ball was dropped, that is,

$$\text{COR} = \sqrt{\frac{h}{H}}.$$

The reason that the COR can be measured in this way is that the height of an object above some point is proportional to its potential energy (mgh) relative to that point. This potential energy is equivalent to the kinetic energy ($\frac{1}{2} mv^2$) the object acquires when it falls through this height. Dividing both sides of the equation

$$\tfrac{1}{2} mv^2 = mgh$$

by $\frac{1}{2} m$ gives

$$v^2 = 2\,gh.$$

Taking the square root of both sides of this equation leaves us with

$$v = \sqrt{2\,gh}.$$

If h is the rebound height and H is the initial height, then

$$v_2 = \sqrt{2\,gh} \text{ and } v_1 = \sqrt{2\,gH}.$$

The ratio of v_2 to v_1 is

$$\frac{v_2}{v_1} = \frac{\sqrt{2\,gh}}{\sqrt{2\,gH}} = \sqrt{\frac{h}{H}}\,.$$

If a ball dropped from a height of 100 cm strikes a solid surface and rebounds to a height of 64 cm, the COR is

$$\sqrt{\frac{64 \text{ cm}}{100 \text{ cm}}} = 0.80.$$

You can determine the CORs of a number of different balls experimentally.

Hold a baseball so that the bottom of the ball is 1.0 m above a concrete or solid wooden surface. Drop the ball and measure the peak height reached by the bottom of the ball after it rebounds. You may have to do this several times to obtain the best estimate of the rebound height. It will help to have a partner when you do this experiment. One person can drop the ball and the other can watch and measure the rebound. What do you find the COR of a baseball to be? How does the COR compare with the value that you can calculate from information given above about baseballs fired against a wall?

In a similar way you can measure the COR of a number of different kinds of balls—tennis, golf, basketball, Ping-Pong, lacrosse, squash, and a handball. Which ball has the largest COR? The smallest?

How do your values compare with those in Table 4 in which the balls were dropped from a height of 2.3 m onto a rigid wooden surface?

Just for fun, you might like to measure the COR of a superball and a ball of modeling clay. What are the CORs of these balls? How do they compare with the balls used in various sports?

Here are some rules about the bounce required of various balls used in sports. Unless otherwise stated, you may assume measurements are made from the bottom of the ball.

Ball	Rule
Basketball	When a correctly inflated basketball (diameter = 9.5 inches) is dropped to the playing surface from a height of 6 feet, measured to the *bottom* of the ball, it should rebound to a height measured to the *top* of the ball of not less than 49 inches or more than 54 inches.
Handball	When the temperature is 68° F (20° C), a ball dropped from a height of 70 inches onto a hardwood floor should rebound to a height of 46 to 50 inches.
Lacrosse	When dropped from a height of 72 inches onto a hardwood floor, the ball should rebound to a height of 45 to 49 inches.
Paddleball	When released from a height of 6 feet, the ball should rebound to a height of 3.5 feet.
Racquetball	When the temperature is 76° F (24° C), a ball dropped from a height of 100 inches should rebound to a height of 68 to 72 inches.
Tennis	When dropped from a height of 100 inches onto concrete, the ball should rebound to a height of 53 to 58 inches.

According to these rules, what are the CORs for these balls?

• How does the COR that you found for a basketball compare with the rule-book value given above? Does it change if you drop the ball from the six-foot height mentioned in the rules?

• It is certain that after 1920 baseballs were wound more tightly to increase their COR. A livelier ball increased home run production, which is what the fans wanted. The standard COR (0.563 ± 0.018) required of baseballs today is based on the result of shooting balls at 85 ft/s (58 mph) onto ash boards backed by concrete. An average rebound velocity of 48 ft/s after the collision is the source of the COR. Experiments conducted in 1942 showed that the COR of these balls decreased to 0.46 when they were fired at the ash wall at a speed of 130 ft/s (89 mph).

You can increase the speed at which a dropped ball collides with the floor by dropping it from a greater height. Since the velocity a ball acquires is proportional to the square root of the height it falls, you can double the velocity at impact by dropping the ball from a height that is four times greater. Do you find that the COR of the balls you tested changes if you increase the speed at which they collide with the floor?

• From what height would baseballs have to be dropped to acquire a speed of 85 ft/s (26 m/s)? Why is the COR of baseballs not measured in the same way as in your experiments? If the rule were modified, could the COR of baseballs be determined using the method that you used?

• Some weak-hitting major league teams have been accused of putting baseballs into a freezer before home games. Could this have an effect on the COR of the balls? You can find out by first measuring the COR of the ball at room temperature and then measuring again after the ball has been in a freezer for several hours. Does the colder ball have a lower COR? If it does, will it retain its lower COR after it reaches room temperature?

Does a warm baseball have a higher COR than normal? To find out place a baseball in a warm (125° F; 52° C) oven for several hours. Then test it. Does a baseball's COR increase with temperature? If it does, will it retain a higher COR after it cools back to room temperature?

Why do you suppose the COR values for handballs and racquetballs were given for a specific temperature? Do the CORs of these balls change significantly with changes in temperature?

What about other balls, such as those used in tennis, golf, basketball, Ping-Pong, lacrosse, squash? Are their CORs affected by temperature? If they are, which one is affected the most? Can you explain why some balls might be affected more than others?

• Can humidity affect a ball's COR? Can it affect the ball's weight? To find out, weigh some dry balls used in a variety of sports and determine the

COR of each one. Then place the balls in a very humid environment. You might use a large sealed container that contains a pan of water. Place the container in a warm place and leave it for several days. Remove the balls, weigh each one again, and determine their CORs. Has the humidity affected the mass of any of these balls? Has it changed the COR of any of them?

• You've probably measured the COR for a tennis ball bouncing from a floor, but tennis balls are used on courts made of clay, grass, concrete, and asphalt. Measure the COR for tennis balls dropped onto as many types of court surface as possible. Are the values different? If so, which court produces the highest bounce? The lowest bounce?

• Tennis balls also collide with rackets. Do you think the COR of a tennis ball colliding with a racket will be different from one colliding with a floor or court surface? Fasten, or have someone hold, the ends of a racket securely against bricks or concrete blocks. Then measure the COR of a tennis ball dropped onto the racket. What do you find? Does it make a difference where the ball strikes the racket? Based on data from this experiment, what part of the racquet should be used to strike the ball?

You might try a similar experiment with a baseball and bat, but be prepared for aggravation; it's not easy to drop a ball on the exact center of a tapered cylinder.

ALUMINUM VS. WOODEN BATS

Despite the fact that major league baseball allows only bats made of wood, relatively few wooden bats can be found in amateur leagues ranging all the way from the little league through college. These teams use aluminum bats. Since aluminum bats seldom break, they are far more economical than bats made of wood. How many times have you seen a major-league player return to the dugout to get a new bat after fouling off a pitch he hit with the one he took to the plate?

There are other advantages, too. Because an aluminum bat is hollow, it can be made with the maximum diameter allowed—2.75 inches (7 cm), which increases the chances of making contact. Most wooden bats are made with a smaller diameter to keep the weight below 36 ounces (1.02 kg). Babe Ruth is reported to have used a 47-ounce bat, but 36 ounces is about the heaviest bat used today. Furthermore, many claim that the hollow metal bat has more spring to it than its wooden counterpart. It behaves more like the strings of a tennis racket, which, by stretching, store the ball's kinetic energy as elastic potential energy during the collision. The aluminum bat, it is argued, allows more energy to be stored and then returned during the ball-bat collision. Less energy is lost to heat and, therefore, the ball comes off the bat with more speed than it does off a wooden bat.

Although it is not easy to do, try to measure the COR of baseballs bouncing on bats made of aluminum and wood. Is the

COR of baseballs on an aluminum bat greater than the COR of the same balls on a wooden bat?

Use aluminum and wooden bats of the same weight in batting practice. Hit against a pitching machine or a pitcher who can throw "meatballs." Measure your best drive using an aluminum bat and your best using a wooden bat. Repeat the experiment with a number of your teammates. Can you reach any conclusions about the comparative merits of these bats in terms of hitting?

COLLISIONS BETWEEN BALLS AND BATS OR RACKETS

When you swing a baseball bat, the speed at different points along the bat is similar to that on a merry-go-round. The farther out you go from the center of the swing, the faster the bat moves. It's like playing snap the whip on ice skates; you move much faster when you're near the end of the line than when you're close to the center.

If you play baseball or tennis, you probably know about the *sweet spot*. It's the place on the bat or racket where, when the ball is hit, the contact feels good and the ball seems to spring away with its greatest speed. When contact is made at some point other than the sweet spot, the bat or racket may vibrate and, particularly in cold weather, may sting your hands. It would be reasonable to think that the sweet spot would be at the end of the bat because that's where the bat moves fastest. But as you may know from experience, hitting the ball at the end of a bat or racquet is not a pleasant experience.

You already know how to find the center of grav-

When a tennis player makes contact
with the ball on the "sweet spot"
of the racket, it usually means
a better hit. Investigate the
physics of the "sweet spot" of a
tennis racket or baseball bat.

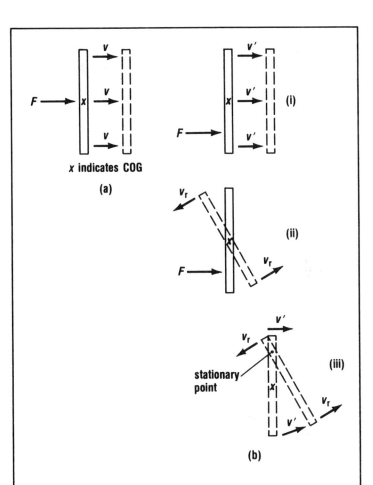

x indicates COG

(a)

(i)

(ii)

(iii)

stationary point

(b)

Figure 20. (a) A force *F* applied through the COG causes the entire stick to move forward with a velocity *v*. (b) The same force applied at some point other than through the COG causes the stick to move forward with a velocity *v*ʹ (i) and to rotate (ii) about the COG with a velocity of rotation v_r. The combination of these two motions (iii) produces a stationary point where *v*ʹ and v_r are equal in size but opposite in direction.

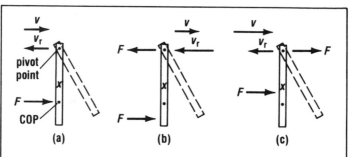

Figure 21. (a) The stick is struck at the COP. The forward velocity v, and the rotational velocity v_r, are equal and opposite in direction at the pivot point and there is no force on this point. (b) The stick is struck outside the COP; v_r exceeds v at the pivot point and a force acts to the left on the pivot point. (c) The stick is struck between the COP and the COG; v exceeds v_r at the pivot point and a force acts to the right at this point.

ity (COG) of a bat or racket. So in the first experiment in this section, you'll find the COG of a bat and/or racquet and then see what happens when they are struck by something at this point.

Balance a baseball bat on your outstretched finger in order to find its COG. Use chalk or a marking pen to mark this point. Do the same thing for a tennis racket if you have one. Now place the bat on a smooth level floor and tap it gently at its COG with a hammer. Watch the way it moves. Then tap it at either end and see how it moves. When struck at its COG, the entire bat moves in the same direction. When struck at any other point, the bat will rotate about its COG.

Try the same thing with a tennis racket. Because the handle of the racket is probably covered with a material that has lots of friction, it's best to place the racket on a very smooth surface. Even then, the handle will probably decelerate much faster than the metal part of the racket, so try to concentrate on the initial movement.

When you hit the bat or racket at some place other than the COG, there is both a motion in the direction of the force and a rotation, due to the torque produced, about the COG. As you can see from Figure 20, there will be a stationary point on the bat where the forward velocity and the backward velocity due to rotation are equal and opposite.

Now suppose the stick is fixed near one end so it can rotate about only this point (Figure 21). If the stick is struck at a point that makes the stationary point coincide with the pivot point, the stick would turn without exerting any force on the pivot point. The forward and rotational velocities would be equal and opposite at this point. The point on the stick at which the applied force will cause no force on the pivot point is called the center of percussion (*COP*). If a force is applied below this point (Figure 21*b*), the rotational velocity will be greater than the forward velocity at the pivot point and there will be a backward push at this point. If the force is applied between the COP and the COG, the forward velocity will exceed the rotational velocity at the pivot point and there will be a forward push on the pivot point (Figure 21*c*).

Hold a baseball bat just below the knob with your fingers as shown in Figure 22. The bat should be free to swing back and forth

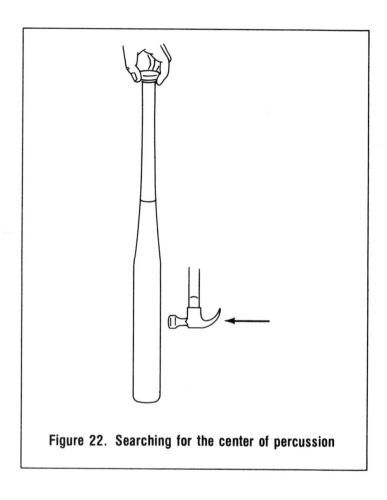

Figure 22. Searching for the center of percussion

in your fingers, which serve as the pivot point. Using a hammer, gently tap the bat near its end. You'll feel the vibration due to the force on the pivot point. Now tap the bat at various points until you feel no vibration on your fingertips. You'll also hear a change in the sound produced by the vibrating bat when you strike its COP. The place where you can tap the bat and feel no vibration is the COP.

Striking the bat at its COP produces no forward or backward force on the pivot point. What happens if you strike the bat between the COP and the COG? Between the COG and the pivot point?

Measure the distance from the pivot point to the COP. Then build a pendulum from a ball of clay and a piece of string. The clay can serve as the bob of your pendulum. Tape the string to the bottom edge of a table. Make the length of the pendulum (from the center of the bob to the point of support) equal to the distance between the COP and the pivot point of the bat. Now set the pendulum in motion. Hold the bat next to the pendulum and let it swing back and forth about the pivot point established by your fingers. How does the period of the pendulum (the time to make a back-and-forth swing) compare with the period of the bat about its pivot point?

Repeat the experiment using a tennis racket. Where is the COP of the racket? What happens if you strike the racket to one side of the COP but at the same distance from the pivot point?

- Find the COGs of an aluminum bat and a wooden bat. How do they compare? How do their COPs compare? How do the COGs and COPs of softball and baseball bats made of the same material compare?
- Test a variety of tennis rackets to find the COP of each. Is the COP of all the rackets at the same place?

If this book has whetted your interest for the science in sports, it has served its purpose. By now you can see that sports provide a rich source for the kinds of questions that often can be answered through experimentation followed by careful and thoughtful analysis. At this point, you've probably discovered a number of your own questions that have arisen in the sports that interest you the most. With the experience you've gained here, you can go on to design your own experiments to find answers to these questions. But don't be surprised if you find new questions in your search for answers—that's the way it is in science.

FOR FURTHER READING

Adair, Robert K. *The Physics of Baseball*. New York: Harper & Row, 1990.

Barr, George. *Sports Science for Young People*. New York: Dover, 1990.

Berger, Melvin. *Sports*. New York: Franklin Watts, 1983.

Brancazio, Peter J. *Sport Science: Physical Laws and Optimum Performance*. New York: Touchstone, 1985.

Frohlich, Cliff, ed. *Physics of Sports: Selected Reprints*. College Park, Md.: American Association of Physics Teachers, 1986.

Gardner, Robert. *Science and Sports*. New York: Franklin Watts, 1988.

————. *The Young Athlete's Manual*. New York: Messner, 1985.

Kettlecamp, Larry. *Modern Sports Science*. New York: Morrow, 1986.

Schrier, Eric W. and Allman, William F., eds. *Newton at the Bat: The Science in Sports*. New York: Scribner's, 1984.

Sportsworks: More than 50 Fun Activities That Explore the Science of Sports. Ontario Science Centre. Reading, Mass.: Addison-Wesley, 1988.

INDEX

"Sweet spot," 115, *116*, 118–21

Tennis, 105
  COR and, 108, 110
  spin and, 81, 93–94, 98
  "sweet spot" and, 115, *116*, 118–19, 121
Terminal velocity, 37
Thomson, J. J., 81, 85, 86–87
Time, units of, 12
Topspin, 103
Torque, 73, 76–78
Track hardness, speed and, 23–24

Unweighting, 49, 51, 56–58

Vectors, 42–45, 57
Velocity, 47, 56
  and force, 30–36
  horizontal and vertical, 64, 65, 67
  and spin, 87
  terminal, 37
  units of, 12
  See also Speed
Volume, units of, 12–13

Weight, 36
  units of, 13
Wind direction, 24–25
Wind resistance, 51–52
Wind velocity, spin and, 90–93
Work, 59–61
  units of, 13